AMERICAN FRIEND:

Herbert Hoover

AMERICAN FRIEND:
Herbert Hoover

By ANNE EMERY

Illustrated with Photographs

 RAND McNALLY & COMPANY

Dedicated to
John Douglas Emery

CONTENTS

Illustrations

PREFACE

IOWA was a special place in 1874. It had become, in 1846, the first free state west of the Mississippi River, and pioneers poured in to settle there.

They came in covered wagons and they homesteaded farms on the Iowa hills and prairies to build the kind of life they wanted. They were looking for freedom to make their way in life without help or hindrance; freedom to learn and teach their children the things they held to be important, and freedom to govern themselves and to worship as they liked. Large numbers of these pioneers were Quakers.

The official name of the Quakers was the Society of Friends. When it was founded in 1652, the society took its name from the saying of Jesus, "Ye are my friends if ye do the things which I command." And of all the commandments of Jesus Christ, the Friends regarded as foremost, "This is my commandment, that ye love one another."

To them, every man was a friend, and this required charity founded on kindliness, help for the helpless, a ready concern for the sufferings and needs of others, and belief in the basic goodness of the individual man. Most Friends refused to bear arms against their fellow men, deeply opposing war and violence. Friends believed that example was more important than precept, and that the chief reason for being on earth was to do good. They put duty above pleasure and integrity above gain. And they believed that every man was responsible for making of himself a person of integrity and independence so that he might be useful to others. It has been said that the early groups of Friends in America were perhaps the best compromise between individualism and community needs that man has ever reached.

Part I

Growing Up

"It is the entry to life which I could wish for every American boy and girl."

—Herbert Hoover

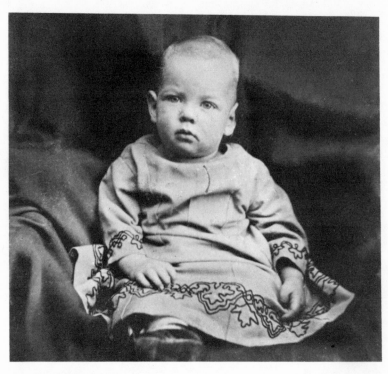

Herbert Hoover as a baby

Cottage on Downey Street where Herbert Hoover was born

ONE

THE little town of West Branch, Iowa, stands on the west branch of the Wapsinonoc Creek, which means, in the Indian tongue, "Sweet Water." It is surrounded by rolling hills, open meadows, and woods. The stage road that ran from Iowa City to Davenport was the main street, in 1874. North of this road children climbed the hill past the Friends' Meeting House on their way to the schoolhouse at the top. South of the stage road was Downey Street, where, next to the Methodist Church, the Hoover cottage stood, with Jesse Hoover's blacksmith shop at the back of the lot.

In the tiny two-room cottage Herbert Hoover was born on August 10, 1874, the second son of Jesse and Hulda Hoover. His brother, Theodore, was then three and a half years old, and two years later his sister, May, was born.

The Hoover children came into the world surrounded by Quaker kinfolk, all of them pioneers.

Great-grandmother Rebecca lived nearby and kept a close eye on her sons, grandsons, and great-grandchildren. She had been born in 1801 when Thomas Jefferson was President. She was fourteen years old when Andrew Jackson won the Battle of New Orleans. She was raising a family of seven children when the Alamo was lost in 1836. And, in 1854, she urged her husband to go out in a prairie schooner to homestead new land on the frontier for the children. She was going on sixty when the Civil War broke out, and she lived another thirty-four years after that: a sturdy, adventurous, outspoken Friend, who gave her great-grandson a heritage of high purpose, a tremendous capacity for work, and an extraordinary executive ability.

Beyond that inheritance, she instilled in him a stern Quaker

13

Jesse and Rebecca Hoover

discipline: boasting and clamor were worldly, fighting back was sinful, being greedy, unkind, or slow to help another was positively evil.

Herbert's father, Jesse Clark Hoover, was Rebecca's grandson. He had an outgoing, kindly disposition, and a fascination with machines and the way they worked. He made some of the furniture for his little home and the walnut cradle for his babies. And when the first threshing machine arrived in West Branch from the East, Jesse Hoover was the only man in town who could figure out how to put it together and make it work. He was also a good mixer, a man who enjoyed people and a good joke, especially when he could tease his serious-minded wife about something.

14

Hulda Minthorn Hoover had come to Iowa with her family of seven brothers and sisters a few years after the first Hoovers arrived. Grandmother Minthorn lived nearby. The Minthorns had been devout Quakers as far back as the memory of their family ran. Somewhere in the Minthorn line the blood of French Huguenots flowed, and some of the French quality of mind and temperament came down to Herbert Hoover from his mother's people.

Perhaps it was this Huguenot strain that made the Minthorns so highly individualistic. Hulda's brother, Henry John Minthorn, made up his own mind about the values of the Civil War and shocked the pacifist Quaker meeting when he ran away to Davenport and joined the Union army. Hulda herself was a strong-minded, strong-willed personality who believed that convictions were more important than tradition. She scandalized the Friends

Hulda Minthorn Hoover and Jesse Clarke Hoover

Herbert Hoover was part of a happy family. In this picture, taken in 1878, Tad is in the tree; his father is standing next to him, holding Herbie; on the right, in the third row from the top, their mother is holding May. Great-grandmother Rebecca is on the left, in front

when she was moved to sing at her father's funeral and lifted her voice in a hymn, an unheard-of thing in the silent Quaker meeting.

She had had a good education, and her family believed, even more strongly than most Quakers, that education was important. Her brothers, Henry John and Pennington Minthorn, had both been graduated from Iowa State University with honors, and Hulda had spent one term there. From the beginning, Hulda Hoover was determined that her boys should go to college.

The temperaments of the strong women on each side of his family were an important part of Herbert Hoover's inheritance, controlling the direction of his growth and his life as much as did the faith they had implanted so firmly.

He was part of a happy family. The tiny house was filled with friends and relatives most of the time. Hulda wrote a friend once, "We have only eaten dinner alone one day this week. Since First Day there has been fifteen here, and this is Seventh Day. I am always glad to see my friends, but it keeps a body busy to keep something to eat, and everything else done up in apple pie order."

The blacksmith business was going very well, so when Herbie was going on six his father was able to give up that trade and set up a business in farm implements. The little family moved into a larger house across the street from the cottage. And young Herbie's life became as busy as his family's.

He went to meeting on First days, where it was hard for a small boy to sit quietly through the long silent service. Unless someone was moved by the spirit to speak to the meeting, the Friends sat silent. Often enough Herbie's mother was moved to speak. Sitting on the men's side of the partition with his father and brother, Herbie could hear her as if she spoke to him.

Between the meeting days he played with Tad and his cousins, sledding down Cook's Hill on white winter days, helping to make maple sugar when the sap was running in the spring. Tad showed his little brother how to catch sunfish with a worm on a hook and a willow pole. And with the other boys Herbie hunted for nuts and looked for stones along the railroad track and sometimes went

17

Herbie and Tad, 1879

out to play in the hayloft in the barn at Uncle Benajah Hoover's place in the country. He had chores to do even before he went to school: he could help to fill the woodbox, weed the garden, pick up his toys.

In the fall of 1880, when Herbie was six years old, West Branch had a torchlight parade for the presidential candidate, James A. Garfield. Jesse Hoover took the boys to see the parade, and Herbie was fascinated by the flaring torches as he walked alongside the parade. He was deeply impressed with the importance of a man for whom all this gaudy celebration was going on.

Less than a year later the flags were flying at half-mast for the murdered President Garfield, and again Herbie heard people talking about the President, this time in hushed tones, waiting while the tidings came slowly and telling each other what a shock-

18

ing loss this was for the country. For the first time the boy understood that some great man, called the President, ran the country.

Four months after Herbie's sixth birthday, Jesse Hoover died of
typhoid fever and Hulda Hoover was left with three small children
to support. May was four and Tad was going on ten. She took in
sewing and somehow she fed the children and kept the home together. She saved for the boys' education the insurance her husband left. And her relatives and friends helped her.

Uncle Laban Miles took Herbie to live with him for eight
months. Laban Miles had married Agnes Minthorn, Hulda's sister,
and he was the United States Indian Agent to the Osage Nation
out in the Indian Territory, now Oklahoma. Aunt Agnes came to
West Branch to take Herbie out to Pawhuska, the capital of the
Osages. There he and his three Miles cousins all played with the
Indian boys at the agency school. Herbie learned from the Indian
boys how to use a bow and arrows, and the ancient Indian lore of
woods and streams. He learned how to fish and build fires in the
Indian way. For the rest of his life he loved the outdoor life.

In 1882—the following summer—he stayed with his uncle
Pennington Minthorn in Sioux County, Iowa. Uncle Penn was
breaking in a prairie farm, and Herbie lived with him in a sod
house. The virgin prairie had never been cut, burned, nor plowed,
so it stretched before him, rippling and feathery, as far as the boy
could see. Uncle Penn let Herbie ride the lead horse of the team
that broke the soil. Breaking that unplowed soil was a moment in
history that he always remembered.

When he went home to West Branch, he was eight years old
and going into third grade. His teacher then and for the rest of
his years in the West Branch School, was Miss Mollie Brown.
He was very fond of Mollie Brown, but he did not care much for
school. It interrupted the outdoor play that he loved.

He was one of the boys now and he could keep up with Tad
and Uncle Benajah's boy, George Hoover. George had gone to a
circus at Iowa City while Herb was away with Uncle Penn, and all
that fall the boys played circus with Uncle Benajah's old white

19

mare. They tried barefoot riding on her back and fell off. They pretended the big yellow hound dog was a Numidian lion and a fierce old tomcat was a Bengal tiger. They put on a performance for all the other children in town who paid pins to get in. But the lion and tiger escaped from their cages and the circus fell apart.

Then in February, 1883, when Herbie was eight and a half, his mother died of pneumonia, and the three children were orphans. The uncles and aunts and cousins and neighbors held council together to decide what would be best for Hulda's children. Mollie Brown wanted very much to adopt Herbie. But she was unmarried, and the relatives agreed that he should live with a family. In the end, May, who was now seven, went to live with Grandmother Minthorn. Tad, going on twelve, went with Uncle Davis Hoover in Kingsley. And Herbie went to live with Uncle Allan and Aunt Millie Hoover. Laurie Tatum, a family friend and lawyer, became the legal guardian for the Hoover children and the tiny estate their parents had left—about $1,500.

Uncle Allan had four children of his own on a farm about a mile north of West Branch. The family arranged with Mr. Tatum to pay board for Herbie at a dollar and a half a week from the little estate his father had left. When he worked during the summer vacation the board was reduced to a dollar a week. Thus, at nine, he was helping to pay his own way.

Uncle Allan's son Walter was Herbie's age and the two boys were good friends. They walked to school together, a mile and a half to West Branch. Sometimes in bad weather they rode double on a farm horse. But mostly they walked.

School was still not one of Herbie's favorite occupations. He had good friends there, he played games and had fun between studies. He wrote an autograph for one of the girls: "To Addie, Let your days be filled with pease, Slip along as slick as greese. Herb Hoover." He did his work carefully and he loved his teacher. But for a long time school was only another chore he could not escape and studies were something to race through so he could get outdoors again.

20

At home Herb and Walter did chores together: collecting fuel from the woods ten miles away on the river, helping Uncle Allan build his own buildings. They brought in crops of berries, fruits, and potatoes for Aunt Millie to preserve and dry. They worked together for money. Uncle Allan paid the boys five cents a hundred to cut thistles. They got two cents apiece for cleaning the barn. They picked potato bugs at one cent a hundred to buy firecrackers for the Fourth of July.

In Uncle Allan's family life was hard and money was scarce. The mortgage on the farm took every extra penny. Aunt Millie wove her own homespun and made it up into clothes for all the children. She made her own soap. Uncle Allan slaughtered his own hogs and repaired his own machinery. And the boys worked right along with him.

But Herb was treated like a favorite son and there was fun as well as work. In the woods ten miles away the boys gathered walnuts and hickory nuts for winter. They trapped rabbits. Herb never forgot the time he let the rabbit get away when Tad told him to hold it while it was tied for captivity. Herb heard about his stupidity for weeks afterward. He was sensitive about humiliation then and for the next forty years.

But the days were too full of chores and people and lessons and the great outdoors for Herb to feel sorry for himself about anything. In the Iowa countryside every day in the year offered adventure. It was a time and a place where a boy could undertake great projects and great dreams, a time and a place of which Herbert Hoover said much later, "It is the entry to life which I could wish for every American boy and girl."

He was growing taller, brown, and strong with the active life. His tenth birthday came and the family began to call him Bert instead of Herbie. A couple of months after that birthday a letter came from Oregon, from Uncle Henry John Minthorn, called John by the family.

21

TWO

JOHN MINTHORN was the uncle who had run away to war some twenty years before. As a boy in Iowa before the war, he had driven teams for the Underground Railroad through which slaves escaped from the South to free territory. After the war he had gone to the University of Iowa and the medical school at the University of Michigan, and he was now a doctor.

Bert could remember that when he was about four Uncle John had brought a string of Indian ponies back to West Branch after a visit to Uncle Laban. He had brought an Indian and his wife to look after the ponies, and every boy in West Branch was fascinated with both the ponies and the Indians, who had taught them how to use bows and arrows.

Uncle John had given up a promising medical career to be a medical missionary to an Indian agency, and he had built Indian schools for two tribes. Now he was in Newberg, Oregon, where a small colony of Quakers had settled. He had lost his only son, and he wrote that he wanted one of Hulda's boys to take the place of a son in his family. He was now principal of the new Pacific Academy, a Quaker school, and could give Bert more education, free, than Bert could get in Iowa.

Uncle Allan and Aunt Millie considered the letter thoughtfully. Bert was like a son of their own, and they hated to lose him. But they could not give him this chance for education, and they knew how much it would have meant to Hulda. They put aside their own feelings and chose what would be best for Bert. He would go to Oregon to live with Uncle John.

For the ten-year-old boy this meant again losing a family he loved. It meant leaving his whole world of Iowa, his cousins and friends, to go off to a strange world alone, to an uncle he hardly knew. He was uncertain what to expect, living with Uncle John. But there would be adventure in the West, he was growing up now, and, though unhappy, he went off without tears, with the Hammil family from West Branch who were emigrating to Oregon.

The emigrant trains that ran to the West had bare bunks and a kitchen stove in each car. Bert carried a roll of bedding and enough food to help feed the entire Hammil family. For seven days he watched western America roll past, too amazed to be homesick. He wrote a letter to Mollie Brown telling her he was disappointed in the Rocky Mountains: they were not as rocky as he had expected, being mostly dirt.

Uncle John met him at Portland without any of the affection Aunt Millie and Uncle Allan had shown when they sent him away. Bert was going on eleven, and his uncle acted as if he were too big to be lonesome or loved. They rode upriver on a stern-wheeler through the beautiful Oregon valley to the spot the Quakers had chosen for their new colony on the Willamette River. Bert watched the scenery go by—needle-leaved pine and cedar and hemlock forests, rushing mountain streams—and he had time to contemplate his Uncle John Minthorn.

Uncle John was a quiet man, not much given to idle conversation, nor to showing affection. He had the driving mental and physical energies of the Minthorns, a compulsion to get done with what must be done, an impatience with inefficiency and stupidity. He had the kindly intention of all Quakers, but it was hidden behind the stern face of duty, and he believed, as Hulda had, that education was the very foundation of a worthy life. He had married Laura Miles, Uncle Laban's sister.

When they reached Newberg, Bert found his Aunt Laura and three girl cousins making pear-butter in a washboiler over a fire in the yard. Aunt Laura welcomed him to the butter-making, kindly but casual, and told him he could stir the butter while it cooked, and he could eat as many pears as he liked. He had never tasted pears before, and now ate pears for two solid days. For years after that he did not care much for them.

He began school as soon as he was settled in his new home, and he began working for his keep at once. He had expected to do that; he had learned very young that in this world a man never got something for nothing. Now he was far away from his childhood and he felt that he must behave like a man. Bert milked the cow, split firewood, took care of his uncle's horses—feeding them twice a day, currying them, hitching them up on call, cleaning the stable. He did not like horses and the dislike showed.

This Uncle John could not understand. His horses were his passion. He had expected Bert to like them too. Bert said openly that he hated horses. He would care for them as he must but he would not ride them. He knew it would have pleased Uncle John if he had learned to love them but he was not going to hide his

The Minthorn house in Newburg, Oregon

The Pacific Institute (Bert's school in Newburg),
with class and faculty

feelings. He did not sulk and he did not argue with his uncle. But John Minthorn grew cold and silent with the boy, and Bert grew more silent himself, performing his obligations without protest and watching the life around him with little comment.

In school he found the work easy, especially mathematics, in which he knew he was doing exceptionally well. This was a source of satisfaction and perhaps he let it show. Uncle John said pride is a snare that leads to disaster.

In between schoolwork and the chores, Bert had time for the outdoors too. He went swimming with friends he made at school; he played baseball, explored the western forests, went fishing and hunting when he was not needed at home.

Sometimes after school Uncle John took Bert along on visits to his patients. These visits meant long and tedious drives, often enough with Bert driving the horses through rough and muddy forest roads. But many a time his uncle came away from a patient and climbed into the buggy with an explosion of disgust over the

25

Uncle Henry John Minthorn

stupid neglect that had made the man sick. Then he talked: about health and sickness, how the body functioned, and how to keep it well. In spite of his usual silences, Uncle John was a born teacher, and Bert learned a lot about physiology on these rides. He never forgot anything he learned.

Sometimes, too, he could get Uncle John talking about the Civil War and the battle of Shiloh. Then his uncle taught him a lot about American and Indian history. He was not so pacifistic as most Quakers. He told Bert, "Turn your other cheek once, but if he smites it, then punch him." He gave the boy another maxim

26

of his own that Bert always remembered: "The meanest thing a man can do is to do nothing."

In spite of the respect Bert had for his uncle's accomplishments and talent, the tension between them was growing. Uncle John had a powerful sense of duty to Hulda's boy, which meant driving the boy as he drove himself: in chores, in schoolwork, and in Quaker routines. Without the warm affection Bert had felt in Uncle Allan's family life in Oregon was hard.

As the boy became thirteen and then fourteen, working for his keep, he felt like a man paying his own way in the world. Uncle John believed the fourteen-year-old boy must be told what was right and wrong and what to do. The boy deeply resented the telling. The struggle deepened as the years went by. Perhaps the conflict hardened because, in the Quaker manner, it went on with few words and dark silences. The day came when Bert stalked out of Uncle John's house to Aunt Laura's father, Benjamin Miles, and arranged to work for him and have his meals there.

Benjamin Miles had even stricter ideas than Uncle John about a boy's growing up. He set Bert to more and harder tasks than Uncle John had done, work that took every weekday moment between school hours. The boy set his teeth and did the work. But somewhere in those years an ambition formed and began to drive Bert Hoover: more than anything else he wanted to earn his living without any help from anyone.

When Bert was going on fifteen, John Minthorn went into a new business with Quaker friends in the Oregon Land Company in Salem, some twenty miles from Newberg, and the family prepared to move to Salem. In spite of the coldness between them, Dr. Minthorn respected Bert's intelligence and ability. He asked the boy if he would like to go with them and work in the office at Salem for a salary of about fifteen dollars a month.

It would mean the end of school. But at fifteen Bert figured that what he could learn in the business world would be more important than what he was getting from the Newberg school. Since Mollie Brown, he had not yet met the teacher who could awaken

Grandmother Mary Minthorn
(Hulda Hoover's mother)

a love of study. He went to Salem with Uncle John's family. Grandmother Minthorn came out with May to live with them.

In the office he did anything that needed to be done: filing papers, running errands, sweeping and dusting, fetching and carrying. He found other things on his own that should be done. He also learned anything he could learn. The Scotsman who kept the books taught him bookkeeping in spare time. The secretary taught him how to type. He helped to draft advertisements. He sat in on the blueprinting of roadways and land holdings. Some of the men in the company were interested in mines as well as farms, and Bert listened to talk of leads and prospects.

His mind was awake now and he was hungry for learning. He

began to think of college again, and when a business school opened in Salem he enrolled for night classes. There he found a good teacher and he went through algebra and geometry and higher arithmetic. About the same time he discovered books.

Bert had never read widely before. Friends believed that young people should read only the Bible and the encyclopedia, and he

Tad, Bert, and May, in 1888

Capital Business College in Salem, which Bert Hoover attended at night

had read the Bible through before he was ten. But in Salem Miss Jennie Gray took a special interest in boys who were working in stores and offices, and she came in to get acquainted with the office boy in the Oregon Land Company. She talked to Bert about books and reading and took him to the nearby library. There she found a copy of *Ivanhoe* for him.

It was an open door to the world of imagination. Bert read, enthralled. This new world became as engrossing as the outdoor world, and he went on reading Scott and Dickens, Thackeray and

Shakespeare. It was the beginning of a lifetime reading habit.

Miss Jennie Gray became, in his memory, another grown-up who was kind to youngsters. His relatives, Mollie Brown, the community of Friends, his teacher at the business college, even Uncle John, in spite of his arbitrary demands: all these grown-ups cared about how he was getting along and offered him something to work with. Their genuine kindness made a deep and lasting impression on Bert Hoover.

When he was sixteen, an engineer from the East, Mr. Robert Brown, happened into the office of the Oregon Land Company and began talking to the office boy. The conversation turned to the advantages of college training for a profession and Mr. Brown told Bert about engineering.

After that visit, Bert wanted to find out about engineering. He talked about it with anyone who would listen. He haunted the foundry, the saw mill, the repair shops in Salem, watching the work and talking to the men. He got catalogs and information from universities and schools of engineering. He visited a mining prospect in the Cascades with a mining engineer. During that trip his imagination took fire: he was going to be a mining engineer.

Grandmother Minthorn must be consulted, along with Uncle John, Aunt Laura, and Benjamin Miles, about Bert's wish to go to college. The entire family believed in college. But of course it must be a Quaker college.

Tad was going to Penn College, back in Iowa, they reminded Bert. He didn't want to go to Penn, Bert told his relatives. They found a scholarship for him at another Quaker institution, Earlham College in Indiana. But Earlham had no engineering courses and Bert refused the scholarship. He knew where he wanted to go.

Senator Leland Stanford of California was founding a university in Palo Alto as a memorial to his only son, Leland Stanford, Junior. The new university would open in the fall of 1891, less than six months from now, and it would offer the technical and scientific training Bert wanted. One of the finest geologists in the country would teach there: Dr. John Casper Branner.

31

The papers carried the notice that public entrance examinations would be held in Portland in the spring and Bert made up his mind to take those examinations. His family disapproved and the boy was obstinate. It was another family impasse. But when the papers announced that the examinations would be conducted by Professor Swain, a prominent Quaker, the Minthorn opposition faded. If Dr. Swain was connected with the new university, it must be all right.

Bert went to Portland that spring and presented himself to Dr. Swain, scared and shy, and knowing he was ill prepared. He took all the examinations. They were as hard as he had expected and he was as unprepared as he had feared. He failed several.

But Dr. Swain was impressed with his showing in the subjects he knew, especially mathematics. He called Bert into his room and talked to him about going to the new university, what it could give him, and suggested special tutoring in the subjects he had not had, with makeup examinations in the summer. He told Bert he could earn his way through the university if he could get in. It was another example of that special kindness of adults for youngsters that Bert had encountered before and which contributed much to the man he became.

There was no telling whether the summer coaching could give him enough to pass the examinations the next time. But it would be a test of what Bert could do when he was determined, and he was going to take that chance.

He set out for California some weeks later, tall for his age, tough and strong. He had a round, serious face, a firm mouth, and great resolution. He was earning his railway fare by teaching mathematics to the son of the Salem banker who was also tutoring for the summer examinations.

All Bert's earthly goods went with him: two suits of clothes, a bicycle he had bought a year before with several months' salary, $160 he had saved, and $50 more that Uncle John gave him.

This was the end of Bert's boyhood. He was going into the world now on his own.

Part II

The Stanford Years

"No student who ever walked its shadowy arcades left behind him so deep an imprint on Stanford life and tradition."

—Will Irwin, *Herbert Hoover, A Reminiscent Biography*

THREE

HERBERT HOOVER found the boarding house in Palo Alto that Dr. Swain had recommended, and tutored for the examinations to be given again at the end of the summer. English composition was the most difficult for him and, when he passed the examinations, just barely, he was admitted to the university with a condition in English composition which he would have to work off before graduation.

With the Salem banker's son, he moved into the men's dormitory, Encina Hall, a week before the hall was formally opened. They were the first students to sleep there. The happiest discovery in the new dormitory was the dining room. For the first time in his life Bert could refuse mush and milk for breakfast.

On October 1, 1891, the Leland Stanford Junior University formally opened its doors under its first president, David Starr Jordan. Just a month and a half past his seventeenth birthday, Herbert

Encina Hall, Stanford University

Hoover was the youngest boy in the Stanford pioneer class of 1895.

In many ways the boy matched the new university: raw, young, pioneering in new directions, uncertain of the future and yet sure about it, facing new challenges with the confidence of the pioneers, looking to the future and leaving the past behind. Bert was tall and slim and had a tough physique. He had an intelligence that was extraordinary but untrained, a mind that had shown before now its ability to cut through nonessentials to the heart of a problem. He was shy and immature with his fellow students, disliked to call attention to himself, was silent but observant. He had the driving ambition to support himself without help and he had the driving energy to match that ambition.

He found a job at five dollars a week in the registrar's office because of his office experience, and he helped to register the incoming class. The twenty dollars a month covered his board and room at Encina Hall. But he needed more than that. Early in the semester he set up a newspaper route to deliver San Francisco papers to the students. Later he added a laundry service for the students. From these businesses his income was increased by a few dollars a month. Tuition was free.

At Stanford Bert discovered a gold mine in learning: an endless well of stimulation and satisfaction. He was free and independent for the first time, in touch with exciting teachers and a rowdy student body, and in that fresh atmosphere he found himself, and

Main entrance to the quadrangle, Leland Stanford Junior University

he found the excitement of using a good mind, meeting challenges, finding the answers to the questions that rose from debate with his peers and from his own eager search.

He made friends slowly because he was shy and quiet. Lester Hinsdale of that pioneer class sat across the table from him most of the year before he realized that he liked this immature, timid-seeming youth. Sam Collins was one who recognized Bert more quickly: Sam, too, had come from a hard-working background to earn his way through college.

Dr. Branner arrived at the beginning of the second semester. He was one of the foremost geologists in the United States, and he was a great teacher who could touch the minds of his students and bring them alive. Bert was one of only eleven students in that first geology class, and Dr. Branner recognized his special abilities—his quick understanding, his remarkable memory, his powers of concentration, and his determination.

When Branner needed a secretary and found that Bert could type, he gave him the job at ten dollars a month. In that job he perceived the special aptitudes Bert had for carrying out assignments. That summer he offered Bert the job of assistant with the Geological Survey of Arkansas where Branner was the State Geologist. It would pay sixty dollars a month and expenses, which seemed to Bert a fantastic sum. More important, however, it was geological experience in the field.

He worked mostly alone and on foot that summer in the Ozarks. The mountain people were suspicious of anyone who might be working for the government, and even a gawky college boy might be a spy. But in spite of their suspicions, he always found someone who would take a stranger in for the night.

Living with the mountaineers, he saw their living conditions, and was appalled. Their diet was sowbelly, sorghum molasses, and cornmeal. They lived often six to a room, tired and sickly, with no ambition. He thought about them quite a lot as he tramped the solitary mountain paths. It was his first exposure to the helpless poor, and while he could do nothing then, he felt a concern for

37

Bert Hoover
as a sophomore

helping them. Such concern centered in the practical consideration of what they needed: better food and education would make
the great difference in their lives.

When he returned to Stanford that fall he was going back to
friends. Sam Collins suggested that he and Bert should rent a
house in town and run it as a boarding house to save money. The
rent had gone up at Encina Hall. Bert moved into Romero Hall
with Collins, and during that year in his company Bert became
interested in campus politics.

In the new university, with no traditions, the students formed
their own organizations. They set up enterprises to publish newspapers and magazines, to present musical shows and concerts, to
play football and baseball and tennis with other teams. They
managed these events to make money for themselves and pocketed

the proceeds. By sophomore year the campus was talking about graft and favoritism and the need for a change. At the same time students who transferred from other colleges to Stanford had brought Greek letter fraternities and sororities with them. In the rawness of the frontier university, the "Greeks" were more snobbish than anywhere else. They combined to control elections, and in the first year there was no opposition. In the second year the opposition began to form and speak out.

A student named Zion announced that he was running for president of the student body. He began to organize the "barbarians" or non-fraternity men and Sam Collins supported him. Bert Hoover went along with his roommate.

Bert had an ideal for a university: a place where scholars and intellectual merit mattered most. He resented the feeling that for the Greeks their fraternity came before their university. When he entered the political battle between barbarians and Greeks for control of offices and activities at Stanford, he was fighting for his first political conviction: that a university should be democratic.

This was his first experience in working with people where he must persuade others to see things as he saw them, where he must argue about a principle and gain support for it. Collins and Zion assigned him the job of getting the vote of "the camp." These were the students who were too poor to live in Encina Hall, and who lived in the row of workmen's shacks left standing after the university was built. Bert had to talk to them and swing them to vote for Zion. The effort was not easy. But he grew accustomed to talking to groups of people, putting his convictions into words, and the very struggle showed his sincerity. The students in the camp liked Bert—he was like them.

In this campaign he met Ray Lyman Wilbur, a tall, gangling freshman who undertook to deliver the vote of the class of 1896. Ray Wilbur was a premedical student and he had the same enthusiasm for science as Bert Hoover. The friendship that began at Stanford lasted all their lives.

At the close of the political campaign, Zion won the presidency.

But the job was not finished. The Greeks had won all other offices and the clubs were still running the activities.

In Bert's second summer Dr. Branner recommended him as an assistant with the United States Geological Survey. He spent three months ranging the high Sierras in California with a survey party under Dr. Waldemar Lindgren, a great engineer and scientist, and a great teacher as well. They sat around campfires at night in the high mountains, or in the homes of mine managers, talking about mining. Bert listened to conversations about engineering lore and practice, gaining more knowledge than a dozen years in school laboratories could have given him.

He rode horseback on the mountain trails that summer and he liked horses no better than he ever had. But he was more fascinated with the challenges and possibilities in mining engineering than before, and Dr. Lindgren became a lifetime friend.

During some of those days on horseback in the mountains, he thought about the Stanford student body and the problems the spring election had not solved. Somehow the activities should be so organized, he felt, that they served the welfare of all the students, not the few who ran them. He came back to the campus in September with a plan for the student body, his first original design in organization: the student body should control all activities, with a student manager on salary who should be a bonded and audited treasurer. The common treasury should collect all receipts from athletic and musical events and pay all expenses. Other valuable activities that brought in no money should be supported out of this common treasury.

He took up his plan with his friends in the dormitory: Zion, Collins, Ray Wilbur, Herbert Hicks, Lester Hinsdale. They agreed with the principle, but they argued and debated the details in long night hours. They compromised some points, they added others, they put the whole thing into the form of a constitution for the student body of Stanford University, and finally they decided to elect men to office who would support the constitution.

They wanted Bert to run for student treasurer. One of his

friends has said that Bert's abilities did not burst upon his friends; they dawned slowly. Lester Hinsdale described much later his recognition of the quality of Bert Hoover's leadership. "Here I was, older, and probably better at expressing myself," he said. "But whenever I came to Hoover with a suggestion or a proposal I found myself wondering what he'd think—and wondering a little apprehensively, as though it were my major professor."

Now after working with him in last year's campaign, one after another of the group found that Bert would be the best man for treasurer, the most important office on the ticket. Bert knew he could do the job. But he disliked the idea of running for a salaried office that he himself had put into the constitution. In the end he agreed to run but refused to accept any salary if he won.

This campaign was more demanding than the first one, and Bert flung himself into it with all his energies. Lester Hinsdale was running for president of the student body, and Herbert Hicks for football manager. The election was so close that a runoff election was held, and the three "H's" were elected: Hoover, Hinsdale, Hicks. The constitution they brought in with their election is still the basic student charter of Stanford University.

Bert set up an accounting system for all moneys taken in and spent, and he published the accounts in the student paper. During his years at Stanford he handled tens of thousands of dollars. He got no A's in his studies and he failed a course in German. But he was gaining experience in living that was as important an education as any academic course.

He was with the U.S. Geological Survey again in the summer following his junior year, this time in the gold-mining districts of Grass Valley and Nevada City. When the maps of the survey arrived from the U.S. Government Printing Office, "Herbert Hoover" was printed beside Dr. Lindgren's name. It was the first official recognition in his chosen profession, and Hoover said later no other honor ever puffed him up so much as this first one.

When he returned to Stanford in the fall of his senior year, he was twenty years old, just under six feet tall, and, in a quiet

Bert Hoover and a surveying squad in 1893, his junior year

way, one of Stanford's distinguished seniors. He was still shy about asserting himself and especially about accepting praise. And yet he showed an audacity of spirit that his fellow students observed with great respect. His close friends, who had come to know him gradually, liked him better the longer they knew him. Will Irwin entered Stanford that year as a freshman and heard of Bert Hoover as a great man on campus. He had a reputation as a brilliant scholar in the geology laboratory, but he was not considered a

"dig": he took part with too much enthusiasm in skirmishes between classes, in managing the football team, in political battles.
He was not "popular" but he was highly respected.

So he went into his senior year working for the university, the
student body, and Dr. Branner. And that fall he met the first
girl he had ever really noticed.

She was talking with Dr. Branner about a rock specimen that
Bert had brought back from the Lindgren expedition when Bert
saw her. She was not only tall and slim and beautiful but she looked
like an athletic, outdoor girl. Dr. Branner turned and asked Hoover
about the rock they were examining and Bert was tongue-tied with
embarrassment. The girl looked at him with real interest. She
had been hearing about "Hoover" ever since she had arrived on
campus. She had blue eyes, he noted. And her smile was "grin-
nish." He grinned back at her.

She was a freshman. Her name was Lou Henry and her father
was a banker in Monterey. She had come to Stanford just to study
geology with Dr. Branner. She loved horses and she was noted for
her horsemanship. And she belonged to one of the most snobbish
sororities on campus.

But she was Bert Hoover's own kind of girl and she recognized
his qualities as he recognized hers. He helped her in the laboratory
regularly. He asked if he could see her after class. He noticed her
in the geological expeditions on Saturday mornings when she wore
walking shoes and vaulted easily over the fences, needing no help.
He learned to dance so he could take her to a college party.

One story has been recorded of her feeling about Bert Hoover
that year. It was said that her sorority sisters objected to having
the student who had collected their laundry the year before call
upon one of them. When they suggested to Lou that this was
unsuitable, she moved out of the house. Whether the story is true
or not, it is the kind of thing Lou Henry would have done.

In May of 1895, the pioneer class of Leland Stanford Junior
University was being graduated. The night before graduation the
class met and sang the song written by the class poet: "The Cold,

Bert Hoover as a senior

Cold World." The next day Bert sat with his classmates and listened to the commencement address and thought about that cold world that lay before him.

Stanford had become his polar star. Here he had found his independence. Here he had found the men and the teaching that awakened his intellect, nourished it, brought it to production. Here he had found the freedom he had never known at home. Here he had met the girl he was going to marry. In all his later years, Stanford was part of his life and thought and effort. Stanford was the home he had never known before.

Now he was going forth, leaving home again, hoping to find a job that would allow him to marry Lou Henry when she graduated. He had his college degree. He had forty dollars in his pocket. He had no idea what kind of job he might find. And no one had told him there was a depression in 1895.

Part III

The Mining Engineer

"It is a great profession. There is the fascination of watching a figment of the imagination move through the aid of science to a plan on paper. Then it moves to realization in stone or metal or energy. Then it brings jobs and homes to men. Then it elevates the standards of living and adds to the comforts of life. That is the engineer's highest privilege."

—Herbert Hoover, *Memoirs*

*Before leaving for London in 1897, Bert grew a beard
to look older (page 50)*

FOUR

IT was not easy to find a job during a depression. Bert went back to the Sierras where he had worked with Dr. Lindgren, around Nevada City and Grass Valley. The Cornishmen who worked those mines were not impressed with a college degree in mining. No one needed Bert Hoover.

Weeks went by, his forty dollars were spent, and the hotel-keeper gave him credit for a while. Bert tasted the bitterness of a man who wanted to work unable to find any work. Finally he got a job shoveling wet dirt and rock into a car at the bottom of the Reward Mine. It was the lowest and hardest job in the mine, and he got two dollars a day for a ten-hour night shift, seven nights a week.

The other miners were wary of a college man working at common labor. Then, as they got used to the idea, they rather enjoyed teaching the tricks of the mining business to the college man. He learned the Cornish dialect and sat around the campfires and the tavern tables with the Cornish miners, listening to their debates on religion, and becoming their friend. Out of every job, no matter how lowly or drudging, came insight and skill that he could use in the next job.

The Reward Mine closed down, and again Bert tramped the streets, touching the depths of despair as he began to think there was no work in the world for him. Again, when hope was almost gone, he found a laborer's job in the Mayflower Mine. Again the boss had no use for college learning. He told Bert that what he really needed was a nose for gold and the only way to get that was to get in there and dig.

By Christmas Bert had saved a hundred dollars and he had

some new ideas about mine work. His brother Tad had left school to take care of their sister May after Grandmother Minthorn died and they were both living in Berkeley, California. Cousin Harriet Miles had come out from the Indian territory to keep house for Tad and May. And Bert decided to leave the Mayflower Mine and spend Christmas with his family.

After Christmas he set out to find a new job.

The outstanding mining engineer on the Pacific Coast was Louis Janin. Bert had met him the summer he had worked with Dr. Lindgren. Now he went to Mr. Janin's office in San Francisco and told him he wanted to work for him. He would do anything.

Mr. Janin was too kind to say "no" immediately. He had more assistants than he could use and a waiting list of experienced engineers. The only vacant job he had in his organization was that of copyist in the office. Bert told him he'd take that job: he could type. Mr. Janin was startled and then he laughed. Bert got the job.

He was in the office, then, when Janin wanted a survey of a mine in the Sierras, and Janin asked him to make the survey. Bert had pushed a car in that mine, and the survey he turned in was so complete that Janin was astounded. It led to another assignment in Steeple Rock, New Mexico, where the Mexican miners were hot-tempered and the problems in supplies, transportation, and water were difficult and tricky.

The mining world was a tough world and, with a rifle alongside his saddle and a six-shooter on his hip, Bert learned how to deal with desperadoes and rattlesnakes. He learned how to solve the problems that went with mine management from waterpower to the handling of men. He learned how to stand by his own reports on a mine, in the face of experts who disagreed with him. And he learned how to live with doubts of himself. He was young and even experienced mine experts often made mistakes. There were days when he lived with doubt and nights when he succumbed to it until daylight. But the year stretched his endurance, hardened his temperament, toughened his determination. He grew from a boy to a man that year in the mines of New Mexico.

After a year of work in the field, Mr. Janin called Bert back to the home office to join the San Francisco staff at $200 a month. Working in the home office gave Bert more free time than he had had before. In college he had been too busy to do the reading he wanted to do. Now he began reading economics, studying the classic economists, and thinking about the economy of his own country. How did it work? What made it tick? New worlds of thought opened up for him about man's work in the world.

During those months in San Francisco he was seeing Lou Henry weekends when he could go out to Stanford and stay with Will Irwin. There had been no one else for either Bert Hoover or Lou Henry since the day they had met during his senior year. They talked of getting married during the San Francisco year. He had a real job now. But she was only halfway through her college work and she wanted to finish. They decided to wait.

In October, 1897, Mr. Janin had a request from a British mining firm, Bewick, Moreing and Company, for an engineer who could go to Australia and advise their managers about the mines there. Janin thought Bert should have that job.

Bert stared at the cablegram in speechless astonishment. Bewick, Moreing was offering $600 a month for a young man, about thirty-five, and thoroughly experienced. Bert was twenty-three. But Janin knew his young engineer was good enough for this job, regardless of his age, and he urged Bert to take it.

Like every other break that had come his way, this one came before he felt ready. It was a great chance, a great challenge. He had met other challenges and he would take this one, too. With the income from this job he could send Tad back to college.

Tad had left Penn College when he was halfway through and had become a linotype operator. Bert urged him to go back to college—to Stanford, to learn engineering with Branner: perhaps they could work together some day. Now he could help Tad pay his way. Looking back on his own college days, Bert thought he had missed some of the experiences he might have had because he had been earning his way. He wanted Tad and other students to

49

make more out of their college days than he had been able to.

He arranged with Lester Hinsdale to receive money he would send back from Australia to be loaned to Tad and others who needed it. He talked over the new job with Lou Henry and before he left San Francisco they were engaged. As soon as she finished college and he could return to California, they would be married.

He was to go to London to meet Mr. Moreing and learn the details of the Australian job. On his way east, across the continent, he stopped in West Branch to see the Hoover and Minthorn relatives there, who were astounded at his early success and this assignment halfway around the world. He crossed the Mississippi for the first time, saw New York for the first time, crossed the Atlantic. He grew a beard to look older when he met his new employers.

In London he was thrilled to recognize the history about him. Here were the very streets Dickens had written of, there were the graves of the Crusaders Scott had described. He thought of Miss Jennie Gray with special affection because she had introduced him to those books.

His new employers discussed the Australian problems without questioning his age. There was a gold rush going on in that wild, half-settled continent. Bewick, Moreing and Company had acquired ten gold mines in western Australia and several other prospects. What they needed was someone to inspect those mines and tell the company how good they really were, and which were worth developing.

American machinery and experience in gold-mining were far ahead of Australian or English, and American miners were considered experts beyond any others at that time. Mining is an expensive venture and, too often, after men have been brought to the site, machinery has been moved in, drilling has begun, and weeks of time have been spent on opening up a mine, it may turn out that there is no gold beyond the first deceptive showing. To determine in the depths of the earth whether the ground holds minerals and, if so, how much, requires not only the kind of geological knowledge Bert Hoover was trained in but also a certain instinct. Louis Janin had recognized this sixth sense in Bert Hoover.

When he arrived in Western Australia, Bert found a flat and desolate land of great distances, dry sagebrush, blazing heat, and almost no water. Coolgardie, the first of the gold-mining areas, was 300 miles from the coast in the Australian desert, and the temperature stood at 100°, day and night.

At the desert mining camp the men were all sure they were going to make a million dollars out of the mine and the air was full of the intoxication of gold. Upon exploration, Bert found the promise was false: the surface looked rich, but the underground levels proved poor and thin. He had to tell Bewick, Moreing to forget Coolgardie.

However, Kalgoorlie, nearby, promised real riches, and he set about developing that mine with the mine managers. There was so little water in that desert that household water sold at two and a half cents a gallon. It was more scarce than the gold men sought so feverishly, and this was a problem Bert had never met in American mining.

He worked out the problem with a filter press of his own invention in which all the water they could recover from metallurgical processes could be filtered and used over and over. After his introduction of this device at Kalgoorlie, it was largely adopted by the mining industry.

When a mine was worth developing, it was Bert's job to plan the development. He had to put together an organization that would work well with him and with each other. He brought in American colleagues—Stanford men he knew well. He was a driver, by instinct, and in the organization he found in Australia he had to recognize the men who would work with him and the men who would work against him. He had to be hard enough to fire the miners who refused to accept American ways and the men who could not work well enough.

He developed the manner of command. He was never a "mixer," and social recognition meant nothing to him. Perhaps

The Sons of Gwalia mine

that helped. Very quickly he became "The Chief" and this title stayed with him in all the years that followed.

He rode Afghan camels from one site to another and he liked camels even less than horses. They made him seasick, they needed more water than they were supposed to, and they liked to reach around and bite the rider's leg if he wasn't watching.

On one of the camel trips he came upon a prospect called the Sons of Gwalia. Welsh miners were working the prospect for owners in distant Wales. Bert camped there for the night and the miners invited him to inspect their workings. It was a small operation. But here, without warning, he found the evidence of a real mine. This was "it"—the discovery he had been looking for since he had reached the Australian desert. As fast as he could get to a telegraph office the next day, he cabled to Mr. Moreing that this prospect was worth taking an option on.

While Mr. Moreing got in touch with the owners in Wales, Hoover spent some weeks in closer examination of the problems, the possibilities, and the costs of the Gwalia mine. He recommended that Bewick, Moreing should buy a two-thirds interest in the mine for $250,000 and find another $250,000 of working capital to bring in men and machinery to expand the work.

Half a million dollars of someone else's money is a lot of money to be responsible for, and it takes a special kind of courage for a young man to advise his employers to invest that kind of money on his say-so. But he was part of the big-time world now, and he had grown hard enough and knowledgeable enough to know what he was doing. Bewick, Moreing made the investment he advised and hired him to manage the mine at a salary of $10,000 a year and expenses, giving him a small interest in the mine in addition.

Hard as the life was on the Australian desert, Hoover loved the work. Living in a corrugated iron cottage, surrounded by lizards, kangaroos, and Bushmen, with only camels for transportation, he could say, "Our staff and I enjoyed every minute of it," and "To feel great works grow under one's feet, to have more men constantly getting good jobs, is to be the master of contentment."

The Gwalia mine was turning out to be as good as he thought it would be and he was passing from technical work to administration. He had to deal with labor problems involving thousands of men, and he had to organize transportation for massive quantities of ore. In 1898, the common policy among employers was to consider workers as a commodity to be bought and sold. Where labor was plentiful, wages were low. Where labor was scarce, they would pay more for it.

Hoover's policy was to hire fewer workmen, pay them the highest possible wages, and cut costs by the use of laborsaving machinery. He declared that contented workmen were more valuable to the employer than unhappy ones. Labor in the mines was not organized at that time and the Australian laborers were fighting for higher wages.

Mining journals and financial pages of London papers reported Hoover's successes in Australia. Miners called him "The Chief," and "Boy Hoover" in tones that sounded like "Boy Wonder." This was the beginning of the part Hoover played in bringing American machinery and techniques to the mining industry of the world. In the next fifteen years he, more than any other man, enhanced the prestige of American mining around the world.

While he was still at the Gwalia mine, a young man named John Agnew came looking for a job. He had graduated from the University of New Zealand in engineering, and all he wanted was a chance to work at any kind of job he could do.

Hoover had the same instinct for men that he had for mines.

53

He took Agnew on and sent him underground to mine. Agnew showed the promise Hoover had foreseen, and within a short time he became the shift boss and, later, mine superintendent. He worked with Hoover until 1914. Eventually John Agnew became the leader of British mining engineers. He was one of Hoover's successes in the field of friends and human relationships which were to become as important as his mining successes.

By now Hoover had accomplished what he had gone out to Australia to do and he was beginning to be homesick. The mines were beginning to pay off. Communities were rising in places that had been unnamed when Hoover had arrived. Agnew was a good superintendent. And the raw deserts, the burning glare, and the rough life were no place to bring a wife. He was thinking of going home for a visit. Lou Henry had graduated from Stanford in June, 1898, with honors. It was more than a year since he had seen her.

At that point a cable arrived from Charles Moreing. Would Hoover go to China to look into a problem there for $20,000 a year and expenses?

Would he go to China!

As Bert Hoover read that cable in a temperature of 100° in the deserts of Australia, no other world had ever sounded so romantic. He cabled his acceptance at once. And then he sent a cable to a girl in Monterey: Would she marry him now and go to China with him?

FIVE

LOU HENRY was the kind of girl who would go anywhere in the world with the man she loved. She cabled that she would marry Bert as soon as he could get home. He stopped in London to pick up the details of the China assignment and then hurried on to America and California.

Lou had been living with her parents since her graduation. She had distinguished herself as a scholar and a leader. President Jordan called her one of the ablest women they ever had at Stanford.

She and Bert both wanted a Quaker wedding. But there was no Quaker meeting in Monterey and they decided to have a civil ceremony. Because there was no Protestant minister in Monterey, the Roman Catholic Church granted dispensations to its priests there to marry non-Catholics in a civil ceremony.

Father Ramon Mestres of the San Carlos Borromeo Mission had known Lou Henry when she was a little girl who rode the hills on a bronco. He was an old friend of the family and he was happy to use his dispensation to perform the marriage of the girl he had known through the years. Bert Hoover and Lou Henry were married at her home on February 10, 1899.

The next day the young Hoovers took a ship for China, carrying with them all the books on Chinese life, history, and customs they could find. From the beginning of her marriage, Lou Hoover kept scrapbooks of her life with Herbert Hoover.

China was in the midst of a "reform and progress" movement under its young Emperor. Bert's new assignment involved the Chinese Engineering and Mining Company, which was to help build a modern, industrial state.

The Henrys' Monterey home, where Bert Hoover and Lou Henry were married

This company owned coal mines and cement plants. Chinese owners managed the company, and they had called in European technicians to operate it. Businessmen in England, Belgium, France, and Germany had bought the company's bonds and lent them the money to open mines and to build ports and railways. Each of the European governments wanted its own man in charge of the technical staff. This would give the favored government the first chance at learning how much wealth they might find in new mines and a good chance to cut in on it.

The young Emperor had appointed the Director-General of the Chinese Engineering and Mining Company, Chang Yen-mao, as head of the Bureau of Mines for the government. Chang wanted a foreign specialist to advise him in the government bureau as well

Herbert Hoover in 1899

The Hoovers' house in Tientsin

as in the company. The European nations were intriguing and bribing to get one of their own men into that post also.

When Moreing had been in China, Chang had asked his advice about the European arguments. Moreing advised Chang to choose an American instead of a European. When Chang agreed, Moreing sent Bert Hoover to him. Hoover would manage the coal and cement business and also the Bureau of Mines for the government.

The Hoovers arrived in Tientsin. Bert set out to learn about the jobs, and Lou began making a home in the foreign settlement. She found a staff of servants, and as soon as the business of living was organized, she began to study the Chinese language. She learned rapidly and well. Bert, who had no ear for languages, never learned more than a hundred words. Lou kept those hundred words in use between them throughout their married life.

Hoover called in engineering colleagues from Australia, geologists from the United States, a harbor engineer from England, and got the harbor works under way.

Laying rails and putting modern equipment into a coal mine was routine enough. But dealing with the Bureau of Mines in the government was a different thing. Within a few weeks of the Hoovers' arrival, the young Emperor had been dethroned and imprisoned, and the Dowager Empress had seized the throne. While the young Emperor had been interested in western ideas, the Dowager Empress wished to get rid of westerners altogether. And Chang, who had been appointed by the Emperor, now wished to please the Dowager Empress.

Bert Hoover saw, in his short acquaintance with Chinese mining, that what the country needed first was a mining law that would provide for equal rights for all nations in developing mines while keeping the properties under the control of the Chinese government. He drafted such a law, providing for government lease of mining areas; for royalties to the government of China from production; for the reversion to the government of any mine after a certain period; and for good working conditions. It was one of the first efforts to protect China from foreign exploitation and still provide foreign capital for Chinese development without loss of Chinese property.

As Minister of Mines, Chang should have been pushing such legislation for the good of China. But he was no longer sure of his job and he hoped to find new mines that would please the Empress and from which he himself could get a handsome profit.

What the people and the economy of China needed was coal, iron, zinc, and copper. Chang wanted gold. So Bert Hoover, while trying to persuade the Minister of Mines to look for the minerals the country needed, found himself instead journeying all over China looking for gold.

Chang had heard of some wonderful gold mines in Jehol, 150 miles away, and Hoover must see them. Bert planned to travel with another engineer and an interpreter on saddle ponies, with a boy and a cook and three pack mules for luggage. But the Minister of Mines must appear with enough pomp so the people would know he was a great man. Bert Hoover, therefore, traveled in a cavalcade of a hundred mules, ten riding ponies, advance heralds and rear guards, a hundred cavalry men and officers, accompanied by a multitude of carts carrying mountains of baggage, and flying banners. It was impossible to move more than twenty miles a day.

The American Friend resigned himself to the situation and took along enough paper books to fill the time. On that trip he read French literature: Balzac, Zola, Hugo, Rousseau, Montaigne. At least the food was good and Bert Hoover was partial to good food. The cook had once worked for the French Legation and he served a five-course meal every night. Anything less would have meant loss of face.

When the cavalcade reached Jehol, a mob of thousands greeted them. They had heard that the foreign mandarin could see through earth and rock to gold beneath because he had green eyes. They trailed his every move while he surveyed the prospect, expecting him to find gold in such quantities as dreams are made of.

There was gold in Jehol, true enough. But not much. Hoover and his consulting engineer explored the surface and the underground mines carefully. Hoover noted that the mills that ground the stone were the same as those used in the days of ancient Egypt. The best veins of gold had been worked out long ago. What was left was not worth bringing in machinery to mine.

Such disappointing news might incite riot in the anxious mob. Bert told the interpreter to tell the crowd that the foreign mandarin's discoveries could be told only to the Empress in Peking, and he slipped away by boat with the other engineer.

There were other expeditions of the same kind. On many of these Lou Hoover could go along. They slept sometimes in wayside inns on mattresses laid on brick fireplaces, they dined on exotic six-course Chinese food, and they wakened at cock's crow in the morning to see a Chinese village coming to life. Lou loved both the adventure and the science. That exotic bridal tour provided some of the happiest memories of her life.

Chang followed up every rumor of a gold mine—in Shantung, in the Gobi Desert, in Manchuria. In the Gobi Desert, the Hoovers found Mongols living exactly as they had when Marco Polo traveled there. But they could find no gold.

A Stanford group in the Tientsin house. Mrs. Hoover is seated lower left; Bert Hoover is standing at the back right, wearing a mustache that replaced his beard

In spite of Chang's disappointment about gold and Hoover's own disappointment that he could not persuade the Minister of Mines to adopt his mining legislation for China and work the iron, copper, and lead mines there, Hoover counted the year well spent. He saw a great deal of Chinese life and government. He read widely in Chinese history, economics, and sociology. He came to know the Chinese temperament and the Chinese mind. And he began to collect books in many languages on China and the Chinese. This collection, later, became the beginning of the Chinese Library at Stanford University.

Little exploration could go forward during the winter. Bert wrote his report on the work of the summer, Lou working with him. She became interested in antique Chinese porcelains and began her collection of Ming (dating from 1368-1662) and K'ang Hse (1662-1720) blue and white porcelain. She collected pieces during the forty years of their married life and the collection became outstanding.

In the spring of 1900, the Hoovers began to hear of a new secret society. The Chinese called it "The Mailed Fist." Foreigners called it "The Boxers." Their purpose was to get the foreigners out of China and destroy every foreign thing—houses, railroads, telegraphs, mines. They planned to kill the Christian Chinese and any who associated with foreigners. By May, the reports of violence were so alarming that Hoover called in all his men from the field. In June he learned that the Dowager Empress was encouraging the Boxers: she, too, wanted no more western influence in her country.

The foreign settlement of Tientsin heard stories of women murdered, Chinese friends hacked to death. A force of eleven hundred sailors and marines was sent to protect the settlement but they had no artillery except two small cannon and a dozen machine guns. Twenty-five thousand Chinese troops under foreign officers were brought up to protect the settlement.

On June 10, the storm broke on Tientsin. Shells burst over the settlement, and foreign officers fled into the city to report that the Chinese troops had turned on them, killed many officers, and

A room in the Tientsin house after the bombardment

were about to attack the settlement. The foreigners now expected the worst. But the attack never came. With no officers, the Chinese troops could not make up their minds whom to obey.

In the lull, the foreigners began to organize for survival. There were three hundred of them, including eighty Americans. A thousand Christian Chinese came into the foreign settlement for protection. Six hundred officials and foreign-educated Chinese joined them, among them Chang of the Ministry of Mines, and Tong, the Director of Railways.

The only engineers in town were those on Hoover's staff. They undertook to build barricades with the only material to be found: sacks of sugar, and rice, and peanuts in the warehouses lining the river side of the settlement. Hoover took on the responsibility for organizing the food and water supplies for almost two thousand people. Mrs. Hoover reported to the doctor in the settlement, learned first aid, and began caring for the wounded in the clubhouse that became a hospital. During that month of siege, sixty thousand shells fell upon the settlement.

Perhaps it was easier to live through the siege when one had to cope with danger and crisis. When things were quiet, there was time to think about the hideous death that would befall all of them if they could not hold out until help came.

Late in July, the first relief forces arrived, strong enough to drive off the enemy and take out the women and children and wounded. When the final relief forces arrived, the Chinese armies were defeated and the siege was broken. The Dowager Empress fled and China was again in upheaval without a government. The Hoovers felt it was time for them to go home and began packing their things. Just as they were ready to leave, Chang came to Bert Hoover with an idea for saving the Chinese Engineering and Mining Company.

During the rebellion, the Russian army had seized the company's coal mines and shops in one town; the British navy had taken the harbor works and coal stocks in another town; the German army held the coal yards in two cities; the Japanese army held the company's offices in Tientsin; the American army had seized the twelve coal steamers. Every nation believed China was falling apart and each wanted to grab its own share of the loot.

Chang's suggestion was for Mr. Moreing to accept a deed for the property and make it a British corporation. The other countries would not interfere with the management of a British company.

Bert telegraphed the question to Mr. Moreing and was told to sign the deed in Moreing's behalf. The Hoovers then went at once to London to tell the partners about the property.

Under foreign management, Hoover told Mr. Moreing, the Chinese Engineering and Mining Company had great possibilities. The coal fields, the cement business, the other potentials could be developed into production that would be good for China as well as for Bewick, Moreing. Hoover was asked to take the position of general manager, and within six months after the end of the rebellion, the Hoovers were back in Tientsin again.

Chinese business custom, Bert found, was very different from western practice. It was not dishonest, as many western businessmen claimed; it was only different. In operating a company, the basis of organization was the subcontracting of all jobs. The man at the top sold the next lower job to a man who sold the jobs below his own, and so on. Each man who paid for his job was entitled to make his living from what he could get out of it. This was called "squeeze," and foreigners usually confused it with graft. Hoover understood how it worked and was much interested in the system. He said there were elements of free enterprise in it. His chief complaint about it was that it was inefficient.

He found that the Chinese had their own interpretation of integrity and in their terms their fidelity was extraordinary. He liked the Chinese for their family affection, their bitterly hard work, their vivid sense of humor, their courage, the magnificent contribution to civilization by the small group of their scholars. He admired the moral strength of the masses struggling with dire poverty and desperate need and wondered if Americans would do as well under the same circumstances.

The Chinese Engineering and Mining Company began to expand and make a profit and, in the fall of 1901, Belgian interests bought control of the business and sent their own man, Émile Francqui, out to China to manage the company. M. Francqui did not understand the Chinese as Hoover did and he refused to honor an agreement Hoover had made with Chang. After a bitter argument about what was fair to the Chinese, Hoover resigned.

He notified Moreing that he was leaving China to return to America. Within a few days a cable from London invited him to become a junior partner in Bewick, Moreing and Company.

He accepted the offer and he and Lou set off for America on the way to England. Both of them by now wanted a home place, an anchor in their own land. They joined Lou's father in building a cottage in Monterey and then they went on to London.

Hoover was twenty-seven years old. He had made a name that was known throughout the world of mining engineers. And now he was to become a partner in one of the most distinguished companies in that world.

SIX

LONDON was the center of the metal-mining world, and Bewick, Moreing and Company was one of the most important and highly respected firms in London. They had operated mines for 150 years, and they held contracts as managers and engineers for mines all over the world: coal mines in China, Wales, and South Africa; a tin mine in Cornwall; gold mines in western Australia, New Zealand, and South Africa; copper mines in Queensland and Canada. They also supported prospectors who looked for new mines.

When Hoover arrived in London in November, 1901, he found that two partners were retiring, Mr. Bewick and Mr. Edward Hooper. Three young partners were replacing them: Mr. A. S. Rowe, Mr. T. W. Wellstead, and Herbert Hoover.

Mr. Rowe had been the chief accountant of the firm, and he would continue to take care of the financial accounts of operations. Mr. Wellstead would be the purchasing agent, buying supplies for mine operations and arranging the contracts on new business. Mr. Hoover would operate the mines both as an engineer and as an administrator. Mr. Moreing, as senior partner, would raise money for developments and negotiate with foreign governments.

The company had to constantly find new mines: old ones were being worked out and closed. To find and open new mines required four kinds of people and work:

> *Prospectors* looked for the mines. They were the dreamers who always thought that tomorrow they might strike it rich. Only a few out of thousands ever did, but among them were those who found new mines, and Bewick, Moreing supported the dreamers who kept looking.

Operators found the money to equip the mines that looked promising. Equipment meant machinery, men and wages for months of work before profits came in, mills for treating raw ore, smelters, hydroelectric power plants, sometimes railroad tracks, sometimes houses, hospitals, towns, and schools for workers and their families. The money came from men who wished to have a part in developing a promising mine.

Engineers directed the actual working of the mines. They found new processes that would increase the amount of minerals recovered from the ores, and they managed the miners, showing them the best ways to improve production and keeping them satisfied with the job, the labor conditions, and the wages.

Promoters came into the picture after the mine was working. When more money was needed, as work expanded, the promoter got the public interested in buying shares of stock in the mine which provided more money for operation. A conscientious promoter gave facts and honest information, but too many promoters promised great fortunes whether a mine was good or worthless and aroused impossible hopes that led to crushing disappointments. In 1901 so many people were hoping to make millions of dollars out of gold mines that they bought shares recklessly, and "promoter" came to mean "confidence man" who swindled the public.

Hoover treated both speculators and promoters brusquely and they disliked him as much as he disliked them. He told them what he thought of their mines and their activities with a blunt intolerance that hurt their feelings and their prospects. When he suspected intentional dishonesty, his temper flared quickly. Among the fringes of the mining profession he was unpopular but he was highly respected, and he was known throughout the profession for uncompromising honesty.

When Hoover came into the firm of Bewick, Moreing, mining stocks were falling in price and stockholders were suing some companies for mismanagement. Bewick, Moreing found some of their own mines in trouble because of poor engineering. Within two months, Bert Hoover was on his way to Australia again to see what had gone wrong with the mines there in the two years since he had left. He closed down some that had run out. He brought in American engineers, and new machinery and methods. He improved the buying of supplies and cut the costs by forty percent. But he raised the wages of the workmen. He had insisted and proved from the beginning of his career that the only workman who made a profit for his employer was a contented workman.

When the Hoovers returned to London in October, 1902, they found a flat at Hyde Park Gate in London. Lou Hoover wanted a place that could be home. Probably because he had, in his world travels, spent so much time in hotels and strange houses, Bert hated them. He wanted his own place and his own things around him. The Hyde Park flat was their first real home.

Once the junior partners were established in the office, Mr. Moreing went off to hunt tigers in Manchuria and Mr. Bewick went to Canada to hunt moose. And then disaster struck the firm.

Two days after Christmas, 1902, Hoover found a letter on his desk: Mr. Rowe had written a letter, twenty pages long, confessing that he had been gambling in the stock market and lost everything. He had taken money from the company and from trust funds managed by the company and had lost that, too. A million dollars was gone, most of it stolen from clients of Bewick, Moreing.

Hoover read the letter incredulously. It seemed impossible. He called Mrs. Rowe to ask for her husband, and she was hysterical. Rowe had disappeared and had left her a letter talking about suicide.

Hoover consulted the other junior partner, Mr. Wellstead,

about the next step. Since Moreing was out of reach, they called in some old business friends for advice, who met them in the Bewick, Moreing office within an hour.

Hoover asked the firm's lawyer to read Rowe's letter aloud. All present heard it in shocked silence. They had known Rowe for years and had trusted him implicitly. It was unbelievable that he had stolen a million dollars. The lawyer pointed out to Hoover that the firm had no liability for embezzlement. There was no obligation for the other partners to pay for the crime of one partner. The London businessmen discussed among themselves what could be done, and one of them asked Hoover for his opinion.

What he would like to do, the young American partner told them, was to pay every dime of the missing money whether he was liable or not. Mr. Wellstead agreed with him. There was a long silence. A million dollars was a lot of money for two young partners to undertake to make good. One of the Englishmen told Hoover, dryly, that he might say every tuppence instead of every dime, and they laughed. With the tension broken, the discussion went on.

Hoover gave a statement to the press that day, telling them the facts, and pointing out that while the firm was not obliged to make the loss good, every tuppence would be paid back to their clients. This statement of business honesty caused a greater sensation in London than the embezzlement itself.

When Moreing got the news a week later, in the forests of Manchuria, he approved of the action and assumed seventy-five percent of the loss, since he was the senior partner and had himself chosen Rowe to join the firm. Hoover and Wellstead assumed the other twenty-five percent. This meant that each paid $125,000 out of his own pocket to repay another man's theft. All of Hoover's savings from his years in Australia and China and most of his surplus for the next three years were wiped out. The story became one of the great legends of business integrity.

Rowe did not commit suicide. He fled to Canada leaving his

wife and children destitute. There he was caught and sent to prison for ten years. During that time Mrs. Hoover gave Mrs. Rowe an allowance so that she could support her children.

On August 4, 1903, the Hoovers' first son, Herbert, Jr., was born. He was registered with the American consul as an American born abroad, and when he was five weeks old the Hoovers went back to Australia, taking the baby along with a nurse.

This time Hoover took an automobile with him, one of the earliest cars to be introduced into those mining areas. It was an improvement over camels and horses but it presented other problems. Sand got in the carburetor, the tires wore out, and the driver was under the machine almost every hour of the day looking for the cause of a breakdown. Even so, the automobile was better than the other transportation. It made 125 miles a day over tracks in the bush.

In 1904, Hoover heard about an abandoned lead and copper mine in Burma. What he heard was so interesting that upon his return to London he sent out a young engineer to scout the prospect. The engineer's report was so enthusiastic that Hoover was skeptical. He sent out C. D. Clark, a more experienced American engineer, to check the report. Clark was even more excited about the Burma mine, and Hoover decided he had better go out there.

Hoover (in cap) with car he took to Australia

He found the diggings, enormous open pits and tunnels which had been worked for 450 years, overgrown with jungle. Most of the works were crumbling, and Hoover and Clark crawled through low tunnels on hands and knees to explore them. Once, a long way into a narrow, low tunnel, Hoover saw ahead of him, in the light of his candle, the fresh footprint of a Bengal tiger. The two men crawled out as quickly as possible, not knowing whether or not the tiger would get to them before they reached the opening. The tiger seemed not to care about pursuit and they got out of the tunnel safely.

Despite the tiger, Hoover had seen what he wanted to see. He found the Burma mine so good that for the first time in his life he put some of his own money into a mining venture. As the work developed, he hired 20,000 people of the poverty-stricken state of Shan at wages higher than any known in the jungle. For thousands of Shans, this was the first money they had ever had, and the Shan State, one of the poorest states in that part of the world, began to prosper. This was a major satisfaction to Hoover in his mining career: that people, communities, and regions should gain new abundance from the operation of his mines.

In the years of Hoover's partnership in Bewick, Moreing and Company he spent more time traveling than in London. He went to the Transvaal in South Africa to examine coal mines and found them underlaid with gold. The gold mining became highly successful, but he was convinced that in general gold mining was unprofitable. He decided that Bewick, Moreing and Company should put more emphasis on the base metals needed in industry: lead, zinc, copper, and tin.

Looking for base metals, he went to Australia to see the Broken Hill operation. Broken Hill was a silver-lead district where earlier miners had taken out the silver and piled up millions of tons of waste full of lead and zinc. Hoover had been doing research with his brother Theodore on the problem of extracting the zinc from the ore and, after a year of baffling effort, they found a method. Hoover purchased five million tons of the waste at

71

Hoover in South Africa in 1904

Broken Hill, tested his processes, and, after some minor problems, he pioneered a new process. Broken Hill became one of the world's richest sources for silver, lead, and zinc.

Part of the success at Broken Hill, as in his other mines, came from his relations with labor. He encouraged the men to form unions and his managers bargained satisfactorily with the unions. He showed that greater technical help for the men meant lower costs, greater production, and higher wages. There were no strikes in any of Hoover's mines at a time when there were bitter strikes and violence in other mines.

Hoover had an immense respect for miners and mining. He said, "Going below after many years of working with the surface people, I have always again the same thrills, the same feeling of separation and safety from the meanness and the handicaps of those on top. It is a curious thing that among underground gnomes . . . none was malevolent, but all were helpful and good-humored. There are no superstitions about devils underground."

It was about this time that Mrs. Hoover found the Red House,

The Red House in London

an eighteenth-century house with a hidden garden and a great linden tree, in the heart of London. All that showed from the street was a wall with a red door.

The house had an oak-paneled library, with leaded-glass windows and fireplace. There was a hundred-year-old mulberry tree in the garden, almost too frail to stand up, which Bert Hoover loved and nursed along with steel supports. In the Red House they could have friends stay and, almost every night, when the Hoovers were in London, friends passing through from China, Australia, Egypt—the far places where Hoover had worked—stayed with them for a night, a weekend, a week. This house the Hoovers kept for almost twenty years, a home that became filled with memories of family and friends.

While they were furnishing the Red House, their second son was born on July 17, 1907. His father named him Allan after the uncle he had loved in Iowa. When Allan was five weeks old, Mrs. Hoover took both boys and the nurse to Burma when Mr. Hoover made his next trip to the Shan mines. On their way around the world, they stopped at Stanford. There they bought a six-room cottage to have as their American home.

During the years of his partnership in Bewick, Moreing, Hoover went around the world five times. He had worked with people and governments in countless countries. He had seen the most glorious scenery the world could offer and the dreariest slums that poverty could endure. He had seen his judgment go wrong on some mines and he had seen it justified often enough to have made him comfortably well-off. He had gone through adventure and through tedious routine, he had seen communities grow where he had brought work, and he had seen miners reject his methods and their own welfare in favor of their old ways.

His name was known in every capital as that of one of the foremost mining engineers in the world. He had accomplished almost everything that could challenge him in his profession. He had fought his way to the top in one of the toughest fields in the world of that day. What more was there to do?

At thirty-four, he was beginning to ask himself if this was all there was to life. He was thinking about what he was living for, and from time to time he spoke of it to his friends. He told Dr. David Starr Jordan, when he met him in Australia in 1907, that mining now held nothing more but money, and he had enough money. He wanted to go back to America and serve his country.

When Will Irwin stayed with the Hoovers in London, Bert told Will that he was thinking about going home to stay. He wanted to get into "the big game" somewhere. Making money wasn't enough.

In 1908, he told the firm he was retiring. Their business had tripled during his partnership and Hoover's share was bringing him one of the largest engineering salaries in the profession. The partners pressed him to renew his contract.

But he had determined that the time had come to live in America. His boys were going to school pretty soon and he wanted them in American schools. He had saved enough money to be sure of a modest living and he wanted more time with his family.

And he hoped that in America he could find a way to serve his country.

SEVEN

THEY moved into the cottage on the Stanford campus and Bert Hoover settled down to spend more time with his boys. But he found himself busier than ever. Many firms called on him to advise them what was wrong with their mines and he set up his own organization to handle the demands.

He did not set up a formal company, but he opened offices in New York, San Francisco, London, Paris, and St. Petersburg (now Leningrad). He invited a number of young engineers to join him, as well as some of the men he had worked with. John Agnew and Hoover's brother, Tad, were among those who joined the firm. Tad had graduated in engineering from Stanford in 1901. For the past five years he had been a consulting engineer of mines, traveling, as his brother had, from California to Burma, from Russia to Australia. Years later, Tad became Dean of Engineering at Stanford.

Hoover knew there were many sound engineering projects that were returning poor profits because of poor management. His men would bring them up to date and manage them efficiently for a fair percentage of the profits. He called his staff "engineering doctors to sick concerns." He said of his organization, later, "Ours was a happy shop. There was the sheer joy of creating productive enterprises, of giving jobs to men and women, of fighting against the whims of nature, and of correcting the perversities and incompetence of men."

He had become the managing director of Burma Mines, and after five years they were still struggling with untrained labor, ground that caved in under drilling, vast quantities of underground water, and tropical conditions. They had begun producing lead from the slag, but they had not yet got into the old mines that promised so much.

In 1910, they drove a tunnel that gave them a glimpse of the bodies of ore, and they were as rich as Hoover had believed they would be. But that tunnel was drowned out. Finally they started a deep tunnel 700 feet below the old workings. It was three years before the great tunnel was opened, and Hoover named it "Tiger Tunnel" in memory of the Bengal tiger in an earlier, ancient tunnel. When Tiger Tunnel was opened, they found one of the largest and richest lead- zinc- silver-ore bodies ever discovered.

The company built mills and power plants, and houses, hospitals, schools, and recreation grounds for the workers and their families. The mines gave a better living than they had ever known to over one hundred thousand Chinese, Shans, and Indians. This was the mining operation with which Hoover felt the closest personal concern, and in which he had put his own money. In 1914, he became chairman of the board of Burma Mines.

During the six years of his American mining career, he spent a good deal of time in Russia, where he was first called in by a nobleman who was concerned with the welfare of the peasants and serfs on his estate. Hoover's men solved the mining problem on the estate and brought money as well as housing and technical training to the Russian workers. In Russia, Hoover saw some of the feudal oppression that was to lead to the Revolution. The people had been oppressed for centuries and he could see the explosion building up.

He was still thinking about public service. But the demands for his engineering skill usually led to improving the welfare of poverty-stricken communities around the world, and he had not yet come to the point where he could pull away from those demands.

He was finding his Big Adventure in making jobs for men, in making something grow where nothing grew before, in discovering the dream not for himself but for humanity. In every country where he worked, he lived with the people, he knew their needs, he brought to them livelihoods with which they could lift themselves above the poverty in which he found them.

Not for Hoover the glamor and splendor of foreign pageantry. He saw too clearly the misery beneath the exotic color of foreign custom. He was working to bring to Australian miners, Chinese laborers, Russian serfs, Burmese coolies, African natives, an experience in free society and the means to live in it.

There was time, living in America, for some personal pleasures. In 1909, he gave a series of lectures on engineering at Columbia University and at Stanford. He wrote a small textbook, *Principles of Mining*. And he became fascinated with a book on ancient mining, *De Re Metallica*, by a German scientist, Agricola, which had been published in Latin in 1556. It was the first written word on mining since the Roman period, and had been the mining textbook for two hundred years after its publication.

No scholar had been able to translate the book because it was filled with technical mining terms and formulas that Latin scholars were not familiar with. Mrs. Hoover knew Latin and she and Bert Hoover began to work out the book together. They carried manuscript and notes on their travels, and for five years it was their hobby. They visited the sites in the Alps that Agricola told of. Lou Hoover hunted through German libraries for books about mining that had appeared after Agricola. They guessed at the meanings of his formulas, took them into the laboratory for testing, and found what he had meant by proving it themselves.

Herbert Hoover's curiosity led him into the life of the time of Agricola and into a study of the historical mining processes. He found that Agricola's processes for assaying, chemical, metallurgical, and mining problems were used by Pizarro in the silver mines of Peru. They were used later in Mexico and then in the Comstock Lode in Nevada.

The book, signed by Lou Hoover and Herbert Hoover, was published in 1912 in a huge folio volume of 600 pages with the old prints and illustrations from the original work as nearly like the original as possible.

In the introduction, filling in some of the background of Agricola, Hoover revealed a deep acquaintance with the culture of the Middle Ages and the Renaissance. The translation and annotation of *De Re Metallica* was an original contribution to the historical literature of mining and the limited edition quickly became a collector's item.

Hoover's interest in history became increasingly important as the years went by. With his collection of Chinese books, he gave Stanford University the nucleus for their Chinese library. He was always fascinated with the evidence of mining lodes that went back hundreds of years, of mining techniques and the stone mills in China that went back to the days of ancient Egypt. Constantly he drew from history knowledge and lessons that had something to say to men of today; always he was aware of the unbroken stream that ran from the past to the present.

The translation of *De Re Metallica* was his first contribution to the records of the past. But his continuing accomplishments as a historian became as important as any other contribution he made to his country.

Stanford University, where his home now stood, was a focus for much of his time and effort. He led a campaign to get a social center for the university, the Stanford Union, raising money and giving both money and time to the project. In 1912,

The Stanford Union

The Hoovers traveled around Europe like any other tourists.
Their companions are probably the Rickards

he became a trustee of Stanford University and served actively until 1961.

In 1912, too, Dr. Branner became an interim president of Stanford. Dr. Ray Lyman Wilbur followed him.

The Hoover boys were attending the children's school at Stanford and they roamed the rocks and hills and explored the outdoor world as their father had done in his boyhood. During the summer, the Hoovers took the boys abroad to see the English countryside, and Hoover amused himself by boning up on the work of writers who claimed that Bacon wrote the Shakespeare plays. He teased the local Shakespeareans with his information and was delighted when the teasing aroused cries of indignation and horror.

The Hoovers liked to travel with friends, especially the Edgar Rickards. Mr. Rickard was an American mining engineer whom they came to know in London and thereafter the friendship was lifelong. They traveled around Europe like any tourists, seeing cathedrals, museums, galleries, and monuments. After all the years of working abroad, these trips were just for fun and the Hoovers enjoyed themselves with all the abandon of holiday freedom.

In 1914, Hoover took his family to London, when he went on a mission for the Panama Pacific Expedition. This event was being planned in San Francisco to celebrate the opening of the Panama Canal. Many European governments were indifferent and Hoover was going abroad to try to persuade Great Britain and some of the other countries to join in the celebration.

On June 28, 1914, the Archduke Ferdinand of Austria was murdered while on a state visit to Sarajevo in Bosnia.

Few recognized at that moment, Bert Hoover no more than anyone else, that this was the beginning of World War I, from which most of the wars of this century have sprung. It was the end of the longest period of peace in the western world. And it was the end of Herbert Hoover's career as an engineer.

Mrs. Hoover in 1914

Part IV

The War Years

"From the rebuilding of the vitality in the children came the great relieving joy in the work of Belgian Relief. The troops of healthy, cheerful, chattering youngsters lining up for their portions, eating at long tables, cleaning their own dishes afterwards, were a gladdening lift from the drab life of an imprisoned people."

—Herbert Hoover, *Memoirs*

Herbert Hoover in London just before World War I

EIGHT

MEN had begun to believe that the twentieth century had at last outgrown war, that this barbaric horror could be prevented by men of good will, and that differences between nations could be settled in rational ways without conflict. And yet the seeds of war were always there. Certainly, when the heir to the Austrian throne was assassinated, the nations sprang to arms as if they had been waiting with guns poised.

When Austria declared war on Serbia, Russia massed her troops to help Serbia. Germany declared war on Russia, mobilizing four million men almost immediately; France prepared to help Russia; Germany declared war on France; Great Britain gave an ultimatum to Germany on August fourth, and called her men to arms on the eighth. Germany marched into Belgium, breaking her own treaty of neutrality with that tiny country. The European continent was at war within a month of the assassination.

It happened so quickly and so unexpectedly to most citizens that it was like the shock of an earthquake. And it upset the civilized world as if it had been an earthquake. Stock and money markets began falling in panic, business slowed down to a halt, ships stopped sailing.

In London, Hoover began to get cables informing him that his employees in Russia were being taken into the army and that banks were closing in Australia, Burma, and South Africa. His managers could not meet payrolls.

The Hoovers had planned to sail for America in August on the *Lusitania*. Now the sailing was canceled.

Hoover was sitting in his London office on Monday afternoon,

August 3, thinking about the personal problems brought on by the war, when the telephone rang. It was Robert P. Skinner, an old friend, and now the American Consul General in London. He told Hoover that a thousand American tourists were milling around the consulate. Banks and hotels were refusing to cash travelers' checks, and the tourists had no money, no lodging, and no way to get home. Could Hoover think of anything to do?

He went to the consulate, a block from his office, at once and found angry Americans pounding the counter, demanding to know if their government was going to protect their rights. It was a disgrace, they said, for American dollars to be refused.

Hoover called his office and told his men to bring over all the gold and currency on hand. He told the Consul he would take American dollars in exchange for his British money and lend the stranded tourists enough money for the night if necessary. He arranged tables for him and his men to sit at, the tourists lined up to talk with them, and in a few hours all tourists had enough British money to pay for the night's lodging.

By the time these tourists were taken care of, the American Ambassador, Walter Hines Page, had asked Mr. Hoover to come to the embassy. He was in even more trouble than the Consul.

Tens of thousands of Americans were pouring in from the continent and all sailings from Great Britain for America had been suspended. Some of the Americans were calling a meeting to figure out how they could get home and Mr. Page thought Mr. Hoover should attend that meeting.

In his talk with the tourists, Hoover offered to set up an organization among the permanent American residents in London to take care of the refugees. By the next morning he had collected a group of American engineers—Edgar Rickard, John White, Millard Hunsiker, and some others—for a permanent committee. The Savoy Hotel gave rooms to the committee for office space and Hoover told the embassy and the consulate to send the American refugees over there.

The strain of increasing calamity during the past days had left him feeling stunned and confused. He found that working with the troubles of other people was the best remedy for his sense of helplessness. He set up committees on the continent to help Americans get away from there, and his London committee found lodgings for them when they reached England and neutral ships to take them on to America.

Mrs. Hoover formed a Women's Committee to take care of women and children who were alone in this crisis. Some of them were stranded without luggage or a change of clothing, and the Women's Committee collected contributions of old clothes for them. Mrs. Hoover arranged excursions to the Shakespeare country and sightseeing trips around London to fill the empty days while these women were waiting for their passage home.

The streams of refugees poured in day after day. Most of them needed money, and the committee cashed checks for them, to be repaid from funds at home. For those who were destitute, the committee raised money to give them outright.

In a six-week period, Hoover's committee took care of 120,000 Americans, including 30,000 teachers, and paid out loans of more than $1,500,000. All of the loans, except about $300, were paid back, and Hoover recorded this later as a tribute to the honesty of the American schoolteacher and traveler.

No one outside of the mining profession then knew who Herbert Hoover was. The New York Times' news story reporting his "admirable relief work" was the first public notice of Herbert Hoover outside of mining journals and reports.

The Hoovers had booked and canceled passage on five different sailings and they now had passage for October 3. A week before the sailing date, on September 25, Edgar Rickard brought Millard Shaler, an American engineer from Brussels, to see Hoover.

Shaler had come to get twenty-five hundred tons of food shipped to the city of Brussels. The people of Belgium were near starvation. German troops had occupied the country since early August and had taken most of the Belgian harvest and cattle to feed their own men. The British navy was blockading the ports of the continent so neither arms nor food should reach the Germans. Within a few days all food in Belgium would be gone.

The Refugee Committee, helping stranded Americans in Brussels, now wanted to get food for the Belgian people. They had already got a guarantee from the Germans not to interfere with food they brought in for the Belgians, and Shaler had already bought the food he wanted from British merchants. But the British authorities refused to let the food go through.

Hoover took Shaler to Ambassador Page, and Mr. Page took up the question with Sir Edward Grey, the British Foreign Minister. The question of allowing food to go through their blockade was vexing and difficult for the British: they were at war and were more fearful of feeding German soldiers than of Belgians starving to death. After some days Shaler got the export permit for his twenty-five hundred tons of food for Brussels. But he was told nothing more would be allowed to go to Belgium.

In the meantime, delegations were coming to London from other Belgian cities, all asking to buy food for their people through Shaler, who took them to Hoover, who sent them to the American Ambassador. The problem increased daily.

Hoover felt that if Americans knew of the tragic need of the people of Belgium, and now of northern France also, public protest would break the blockade. He talked with his friend Melville E. Stone, the general manager of the Associated Press, who was in London at the time. Stone gave instructions to the AP men in London, Berlin, and Brussels to get the rest of the story and give it to the American papers.

October 3 had come and gone. Mrs. Hoover sailed for home with the boys since it was time for them to be in school. Mr. Hoover had canceled his sailing so that he could continue to work on the Belgian problem with Shaler. After giving the story to Mr. Stone, he felt he had done what he could and he made another sailing reservation for October 25.

He had worried about his family's crossing, because Herbert Jr. had expected to be seasick. When Mrs. Hoover cabled back to say that young Herbert had eaten seven cream puffs in one day during the voyage, his father stopped worrying. The British censor thought the cable was some kind of code and muttered threatening warnings about what happened to spies.

Hoover settled down to wait for his own sailing date. He was staying at the Red House and Will Irwin was staying with him. Irwin was now one of the most important American war correspondents. Hoover talked with his old friend about the problems the war had brought to him. His business interests were in such upheaval he could not tell whether he had any business left or not. One day he remarked to Will that he wasn't worrying about making a living. He could always get fees as a consultant. But his savings were gone and he'd had plans for them. They would have allowed him to go into public service as he had been thinking of doing. Now it looked as if the public service might have to be deferred again.

The week before his sailing date, Mr. Page called Hoover to the American Embassy again. Belgian officials were asking to see him. One of them was Émile Francqui, with whom Hoover had quarreled fourteen years before over the management of the Chinese Mining and Engineering Company. Francqui was now a leading Belgian banker, and Hugh Gibson, First Secretary of the American Ministry in Brussels, was with him. This time it was really a question of life or death for the people of Belgium and northern France.

Francqui wanted Hoover to undertake the problem of feeding Belgium. Such an administrator must be neutral and must have the confidence of the American Ambassador. Hoover was the only man who could do the job, Francqui said. He himself would serve in any way Hoover wished or he would withdraw.

Hoover listened to him, troubled and thoughtful. His own instinct was to help people. But this time he wondered if it were possible. He would have to find a food supply great enough to feed ten million people every day. He would have to find ships, trucks, and trains to carry those tons of food every day so long as the war went on. He must find money to pay for both food and shipping. The British navy would try to stop the food from reaching enemy territory, the German army would try to take the food for their own hungry people. Someone would have to distribute the food so that everyone got a fair share. Feeding an entire nation . . .

He told Francqui he must have time to think about the problem before he said either yes or no. When he got home, he talked with Irwin about the bewildering details.

He'd have to give up his mining business for the duration of the war. His mind was already sorting out requirements and plans. If he tried to stay in business, too many people on both sides were going to think he was doing the job of feeding Belgium for business advantage . . . so he didn't know what he was going to do.

He walked the floor at night, jingling coins in his pocket as he often did when he was deep in thought. Even if it were possible to feed Belgium, it could not be done by one man alone. He'd have to find people to work with him. And he still had his personal responsibilities to his managers, his workers, and his clients. He spent a day consulting his associates and cabling his clients, asking their opinions. They all agreed that his engineering colleagues could handle the business problems if Hoover would help with major decisions.

He was at the top of his career in 1914. Zinc and lead would be fabulously valuable if the war went on. With the mines he controlled, he could become one of the wealthiest men in the world. But the Friend shied away from the thought of making a fortune out of the tragedies of war.

He came down to breakfast the next morning to find Irwin at the table. Hoover filled his plate, poured his coffee, sat down, and sipped it in thoughtful silence. He looked at Irwin. "Well," he said, "let the fortune go to hell!"

After breakfast he met with the Belgian officials and told them he would take on the job they had asked him to do.

NINE

THAT same evening Hoover called eight men to meet with him in his office the next morning: Millard Hunsiker, John White, Edgar Rickard, Millard Shaler, John Lucey, who were all American engineers; Hugh Gibson of the legation in Belgium; Ben S. Allen, of the Associated Press; and an American banker who quickly dropped out of the group.

When the nine men met the next morning, the Commission for the Relief in Belgium was formed: CRB. They planned the organizational details so they could begin work immediately: John Lucey would open a shipping office in Rotterdam; Edgar Rickard would manage the London office; Hugh Gibson would be diplomatic adviser, since the work would require dealing with governments; John White would take care of purchasing the food supplies and finding the shipping for them; Millard Shaler would manage the Brussels office. Finally, Hoover cabled Lindon Bates to open a New York office.

No one thought the war would last beyond the next summer. If they could carry the Belgians through the eight months until harvest, they were sure the little country could get along on its own after that.

They established the policies of the CRB: they would organize the charity of the world through public opinion; they would get an American volunteer staff for the work in Belgium; they would have on their letterhead all the American ambassadors and ministers in Europe, and also the important neutrals, to assure both Allies and Germans that this was a neutral effort.

Hoover's personal policy was to accept no salary or remuneration, and many of his colleagues followed his example.

John White said, "We're about to handle millions of dollars. Some day some swine will rise up and say we either made a profit out of this business, or that we stole the money."

The Commission engaged the leading British firm of auditors to keep their books and account for every cent that came in and went out.

Through their own wide-flung connections, Hoover and the other engineers telegraphed friends to set up CRB committees around the world. Forty of the American states set up state committees. CRB committees sprang up in Australia, New Zealand, South Africa, Canada, Japan, and most of the Latin American countries.

Hoover issued a call to young Americans who were willing to work for a bare living and the satisfaction of saving life. American youth poured in to the CRB offices until there were more volunteers than openings.

Within a week after that first meeting, twenty thousand tons of wheat and other supplies were picked up in Holland by the CRB and delivered to Belgian cities by Dutch canals which were not blockaded. Within six weeks they had delivered another sixty thousand tons of food from overseas. Then Hoover went to Belgium himself to see how the machinery of distribution was going to work.

Seeing with his own eyes the stricken land, the streets empty of children, the bleak, unsmiling people, he realized that the CRB must provide more than bare essentials. There must be enough food, properly balanced, to keep the people healthy, and it was going to take more food and more money than they had first estimated.

Will Irwin had gone back to New York to write stories about Belgium that would arouse American sympathy and generosity. Newspapers and magazines recognized the appeal of the big story and kept trying to get personality reports on Hoover that would make him a hero. He was disturbed about that. He said, "Play up the need in Belgium and keep me out of it." But the correspondents could not be kept from writing stories about Hoover and his fame was growing. He was affronted: he thought it looked as if he were using the misery of ten million people to make a hero out of himself.

He was keeping himself in the background as much as possible. But when the CRB was close to collapse in January, 1915, and the time had come to get support from the warring governments, Hoover went to the British Prime Minister, Herbert Asquith, to persuade Great Britain to help in the effort to save Belgium.

Winston Churchill, the First Lord of the Admiralty, and Lord Kitchener, the Minister of War, were opposed to the whole idea of feeding the Belgians. The military leaders considered that if the Belgians starved it would hurt the Germans in the eyes of the world and help the Allies to win the war.

Hoover persuaded Sir Edward Grey to let him meet with the British cabinet and explain what CRB was doing. After his presentation, they agreed reluctantly to open the blockade to food shipments, but only if CRB could guarantee that the Germans got none of the food. Hoover could not then make this guarantee but immediately went to work on it.

He gave a story to the press explaining how much money was needed to keep the Belgians from starving and how the Germans were draining off food and money from the tiny country they had invaded. The day after he sent the story to the papers, he went to Berlin to talk to the German government.

They listened to his argument, because, above all, the German officials did not want the American people to be unfriendly to Germany. They were genuinely fearful that the CRB might place behind their lines thousands of spying eyes and secret agents. Hoover guaranteed the neutrality and discretion of his workers. He also reminded the Germans again that America would turn against them if Belgium starved.

The German official staff agreed to stop taking food from Belgium; to let the American staff come and go without search; to order their submarine commanders not to fire on American

or CRB ships; and they agreed to give some financial aid to CRB.
The negotiation had been successful.

But Hoover discovered something else in that trip to Berlin
that was important and frightening. He had seen total war for
the first time: the entire civilian population drafted into the business of producing food and munitions of war. This was something
the world had not seen since ancient Sparta. He went back to
London, knowing now that the war would not be over by harvest.
It had not yet really begun.

With a written, signed German agreement in hand, Hoover
pointed out to the British government that if the world thought
Great Britain was starving Belgium, it would be the surest way
for the Allies to lose American sympathy. The British Cabinet
now agreed to open the blockade to CRB shipments and to
contribute £1,000,000 a month to CRB.

The negotiations with France were difficult and discouraging.
But, in the end, France, too, sent $3,000,000 a month to CRB.
With financial support assured, the CRB could turn its attention
to all the other problems.

The problems were all new. There had never in history been
a situation like the Belgian tragedy. Industry had collapsed soon
after the invasion. Half of the people were out of work and penni-
less. Some people were still well-to-do but their money could buy
nothing. The important thing in food administration was that
everyone should share and fare alike, regardless of their means.

The CRB set up ration cards for the whole population, with
punch squares marked for days and weeks. Separate cards were
issued for each major food commodity, one to a family, or to a
single person living alone. When a family got its allotment of
bread for a day, the card was punched. When they got their
sugar for the week, the card was punched.

The program was neither welfare nor charity. The commission
divided the people into two groups: those with money to pay for
their food, who needed "Provisioning"; and those who needed
"Benevolence" because they were destitute. "Provisioning" rations

were sold for cash at the same price to everyone who could pay. The money from "Provisioning" paid for "Benevolence."

As the program developed, the CRB was operating flour mills, bakeries, dairies, slaughterhouses, restaurants, and all other places in which food was processed. This provided jobs for unemployed Belgians.

When the CRB found that growing children needed a special diet to fight off disease, they invented a cookie containing fats, sugar, cocoa, and every other food chemical essential for growing children. They manufactured this in great quantity and served

A soup kitchen for children in a Belgian school

it every day with stew and milk to two and a half million children. The fading children revived quickly. For Hoover it was the great joy of the whole effort to watch the children grow cheerful and noisy again.

Mrs. Hoover had brought their own boys back to London in the fall of 1915 to be with their father. She entered them in school and began relief work herself. With other American women she helped establish a knitting factory for unemployed British women, developed a rehabilitation program for the wounded, set up a relief organization for soldiers' wives in need, and worked in the hospital.

Hoover was working at such speed, between the crises in diplomacy, in shipping, in finances, that his friends worried about him. It seemed impossible that any man could so drive himself without breaking down. But the physique he had developed in his younger outdoor days could take whatever pressures he put upon it.

However, when a lull in emergencies came, he relaxed and put the problems out of his mind. The chief source of refreshment for Hoover, since the early days of his boyhood, was to be in touch with the earth, out in the open, with the sky and the trees and the wind. Often in those hard days, he'd take a day off, collect some primitive cooking equipment, and take his family and a couple of old friends out into the English countryside. In some spot, as nearly wild as the country offered, he'd build one of his Indian fires, in which he had always taken pride, and cook bacon and eggs for the party. And lounging against a tree, he'd talk—about college days, about adventure in China, about politics and science. He would also relate anecdotes of the Australian days. He was a great conversationalist and a good storyteller when he was in a small group of close friends.

When Hoover's work took him to the continent more and more often, and the boys began talking with an Oxford accent, Mrs. Hoover took them back to America to stay.

Meanwhile the work of the CRB was expanding, and the cash receipts from "Provisioning" became larger than "Benevolence" needed. The CRB now paid teachers' salaries to keep the schools open and cooperated with police and judges to run the communities; they bought fuel, clothes, rent, and medical care as well as food for "Benevolence." They paid for hospitals and other institutions. Beyond feeding the people, CRB was helping the entire country to keep running.

Over fifty thousand Belgian and French women worked for CRB and were paid with free rations. They cooked for the soup kitchens and Hoover reported they were all great cooks. They took such pride in their soup that they insisted he should sample some from each kettle. They organized workrooms to repair, make over, and distribute used clothing to the needy. They saved the lace industry of Belgium.

For over a hundred years the Belgian lace makers had led the world in their art. There was no market for lace in wartime, and if years passed, during which the lace makers could not work, the art would be lost forever. The "Benevolence" women arranged with Hoover to buy the lace with ration cards. Each piece was marked with the maker's name and carefully stored until the war was over. The ladies told Hoover the lace could be sold for cash after the war. He was skeptical about that but he did feel that it was important to keep the art of making lace alive. To his astonishment, when the war was over, the lace was sold for enough money to pay each of the makers a good price.

The business of feeding ten million people in enemy-occupied territory was working efficiently but it never became easy. Both sides harrassed the CRB with constant suspicion. And at home, in America, Senator Henry Cabot Lodge, Sr., attacked the CRB as an American entanglement in foreign wars.

Hoover sailed for New York in May, 1915, to deal with this attack. The good will of a neutral United States was CRB's most important asset.

He talked first with Melville Stone of the Associated Press, who gave a dinner for two hundred of the leading newspapermen of New York so Hoover could talk to them about CRB. Then he

European women embroidered
the flour sacks that came from
America and sent them back
as an expression of their appreciation. Many of them are
on display in the Thank You
Room of the Herbert Hoover
Library in West Branch, Iowa

talked with President Woodrow Wilson and with former President
Theodore Roosevelt. All were solidly behind the CRB. Assured
of this support, he went to call upon Senator Lodge.

The senator accused Hoover of making agreements with a foreign government which might involve the United States in the
war. He pointed out that there was a law—the Logan Act—that
made such activity a penitentiary crime.

Hoover knew the law. He explained he was not acting as a
private citizen but as head of a neutral organization. He pointed
out that he was sure the American people were in favor of saving
the lives of ten million people even if it did involve the Logan Act.
Finally he told Senator Lodge that he had given the story to the
press at a public dinner, and the press was strongly interested in
arousing public opinion to support the CRB. Senator Lodge
backed down, saying he had not known the facts, and Hoover
knew there would be no further opposition there.

Certainly the American people were behind Belgian Relief.
From every village and farm contributions flowed in a steady
stream. States sent "state food ships" to Belgium. Shiploads of
used clothes went out from American homes. The very business
of making these contributions had aroused compassion and sympathy around the United States for the Belgian people, and Hoover returned to London knowing that his countrymen would support his work more strongly than ever.

During those months he crossed the North Sea forty times to
settle some crisis either in England or on the continent. On each
crossing he risked being blown up by mines or submarines. No
single day went by without a struggle to keep some part of the
mechanism from breaking down.

And yet, in the midst of crisis, emergency, and conflict, Hoover
saw clearly the historical importance of the war he was involved in.
When the first agents of the CRB went into Belgium, he asked
them to collect the fugitive materials of history for him: the proc-
lamations and pamphlets, government orders, newspapers, magazines, books and letters, posters—any scraps that might record some

action or feeling about the war. These were the things that contained the very life of history, and these were the things that disappeared most quickly and were lost forever.

During those early months he was still concerned about his professional obligations. But as the months went by he realized that he could make only one decision. In 1916 he resigned from every business connection except the board of Burma Mines to clear his time and his mind for uninterrupted work with the CRB.

He was doing this complex and frustrating job because he wished to serve humanity. From the day he agreed to head the commission he never accepted a dollar in payment for service or for travel. His associates followed his example, and they contributed money so that others, who had no private means, could also work with Hoover.

When the auditors presented their complete report in 1919, it showed that less than one-half of one percent of the CRB money had been used for administrative expense. The auditors themselves gave their services without remuneration, following Hoover's example, and recorded in their final certificate, "We consider it an honor to have been selected as auditors of the Commission, and to have been able to make a contribution to so great a work . . . no profit whatever accrued to our firm as a result of the arduous services rendered by our firm over a long term of years."

TEN

DURING the early years of the war, the Allies had hoped that the United States would enter the war on their side. Germany had hoped the United States would stay neutral. From the beginning Hoover opposed American entry into the war. He knew the power politics on both sides and he believed that America could neither change the European powers nor make a lasting peace by taking part in the war.

But, in January, 1917, Germany announced that she would sink without notice any ships she could reach on the seas. The American government broke off diplomatic relations and began to arm her merchant ships. In March, Germany sank four American merchant ships. This was a direct attack upon the United States.

Hoover knew his country would soon be at war with Germany and he would, therefore, have to turn the direction of the CRB over to neutral nations. For him this was a personal loss. He cared so much about the people he had been working and fighting for that giving them over to other hands cast him into a black depression which his friends observed with concern.

However, he moved promptly to find a successor. The Spanish and Dutch governments agreed to work together to carry on the work of CRB.

America declared war on Germany on April 6, 1917, and President Wilson called Hoover home to take charge of food organization in America. The President knew, as Hoover knew, that America must now provide food for her own armies and those of the other Allies, for the Allied people behind the lines, for the occupied countries, and for the American people at home.

Three hundred million people were looking to America for food.

Newspapers carried stories about the need for a "Food Dictator" or the "Food Czar." Hoover wanted no such titles. He told the press the basis for the whole effort must be the willingness of the people to serve the interests of the nation voluntarily, and the best title for his new position would be "Food Administrator." He believed that the American people would respond to the call for their help without laws or compulsion. His faith in the American people's voluntary cooperation has been called courage. The courage was firmly grounded in his insight into the American spirit.

Ray Lyman Wilbur, now the president of Stanford University, and others who had worked with Hoover in CRB came to Washington to ask to help him again. Within a few days he had the basic personnel for the Food Administration program. They were men of the same caliber as those who had worked with him in Belgium.

According to Hoover's plan, Americans at home would have to eat according to a program that would leave more essential foods to be shipped abroad. Nothing could be wasted. Farmers must grow bigger crops, raise more pigs. Prices must remain steady. There must be no profiteering, no hoarding. No one, at home or abroad, should lack any essential food.

Signs and posters went up across the country—in homes, stores, on billboards: "Food Will Win the War." Stories told of the food needs of the world, and how the Food Administration could supply them. The American people responded magnificently.

Hoover ordered all press releases to publicize the cause and not the man: news stories should speak of "The United States Food Administration" or "The Food Administrator," never "Mr. Hoover." But the American people knew who Mr. Hoover was: he was the man who was feeding the world and they were helping him.

Americans made games and contests out of the job of con-

102

Herbert Hoover, when he was Food Administrator

serving food. A milling company held a contest for cornbread recipes, to conserve wheat. Cooking pages in magazines carried new recipes for corn and fish and syrups, to conserve wheat and meat and sugar. Every child learned to clean his plate. *Life* Magazine advised, "Do not permit your child to take a bite or two from an apple and throw the rest of it away. Nowadays even children must be taught to be patriotic to the core," and the nation smiled.

The Food Administrator called his program "food conservation." Millions of citizens called it "Hooverizing" and outdid themselves to follow his every request. Routinely, the people observed wheatless Mondays and Wednesdays, meatless Tuesdays, porkless Thursdays and Saturdays. As a result of the increased production of the farmers and the enthusiastic sacrifice and conservation by the people, America shipped to the Allied countries the food that kept them fighting. It was a weapon second only to munitions.

In the last year of the war—1917–18—the Allies were again arguing about the food blockade, wishing to use food as a weapon. Some of them believed that if they starved the German women and children at home, the German armies would give up and go home to take care of their families.

From the beginning, Hoover had fought the idea of starving civilians to win a war. German women and children were people, too, and he showed President Wilson a plan for feeding the hungry women and children of Germany without helping Germany's military position. Wilson was sympathetic. The other Allies were appalled. Feeding the enemy, indeed!

Hoover wasted no breath in arguments about decency and charity: the men at war would not hear them. He said again and again that stunted bodies and deformed minds in the next generation were poor foundations upon which to rebuild civilization. A sickly and warped generation after this war could not keep the peace.

No one heard that argument, either.

Now that Hoover was living in Washington, Mrs. Hoover found a pleasant house there and brought the boys from California. Herbert Junior was fourteen that year and Allan was eleven. After the years of separation, the Hoovers could live together again.

In spite of long hours on the job, Mr. Hoover could spend weekends with his family. During the summer they went on picnics with the Rickards and other families of the Food Administration personnel. They cooked lunches over campfires, and Mr. Hoover showed the children how to build dams and canals in the brooks and how to make boats sail in the pools. He loved to do things with his hands as much as the children did.

Winter weekends they drove out to snowfields and skating ponds, where grown-ups built bonfires to keep warm while the children skated and tobogganed. And, as always, in the Hoovers' home, they had visitors and guests constantly. During the war years, Marshal Joffre, Ignace Jan Paderewski, Thomas Masaryk, and Arthur Balfour were among them—some as official guests, but most as old friends.

The boys went to the Friends' school in Washington, and Mrs. Hoover began working for the girls who swarmed into the city for war jobs. There were so many new employees that many of them could find no place to live. Mrs. Hoover, with some of the other wives, organized a Girls' Club, where the girls could get temporary living quarters until they could find permanent ones.

The Food Administration wives managed a cafeteria in the Food Administration building so well that people from all government buildings came there for food that was both cheap and good. In spite of the low prices, the wives made a profit on the operation, and this they used for other benefits for the women employees in Washington. In every public effort her husband undertook, Lou Hoover found something that a woman could do to contribute toward its total success.

The United States had been at war for eighteen months when

the German armies finally faced defeat in the fall of 1918 and asked for an armistice: an end of fighting while peace terms could be discussed. The armistice was proclaimed on November 11, 1918.

Before the armistice, Hoover had been making a survey to find out how much food would be needed for the coming year. By now, Herbert Hoover knew more about buying, processing, shipping, and distributing food supplies than any other man in the world. Six days after the armistice he sailed with his staff for Europe to continue fighting starvation. That battle would have to go on beyond the armistice and beyond the peace. America must feed the countries devastated by war until they could feed themselves again.

Hoover found Europe dizzy with joy at the end of the war. The men were coming out of the trenches, throwing away their guns, going home again. The killing had ended.

The German Kaiser, the emperors and dictators—all the leaders who had taken the countries into war were overthrown. In Russia, the Czar had been killed in the Revolution and the people looked forward to a free land. War must never happen again. The peace which was going to bring all the nations together in friendship would be beautiful.

But the glory quickly faded as the world began to count the cost of the war. Homes were shattered, family life was destroyed, continuing famine beat down the people. Ten million men had been killed or crippled; another ten million had died of disease or starvation. There was no industry, no business, no manufacturing, no jobs for the men coming home, no money.

The people began to remember what had happened in the war, and peace wasn't enough. They began to hate again and they wanted revenge. The men who made the war should pay for it. And Russia, which had fought with the Allies in the beginning, had already lost her Revolutionary freedom to Communism.

When Hoover met with the ministers of European Allies the day after his arrival in Paris, all the selfishness and rivalry and suspicion he had worked against in the earlier years were still there. The sufferings of the war had not changed the leaders' goals of national prestige and power. The statesmen of England, France, and Italy wanted to use food for bargaining at the peace table. They wanted to hold up food supplies to liberated and neutral countries until they could gain advantages from them.

Hoover told the Allied ministers that after only a few months without food, the lives of tens of millions of children would be stunted and warped. They could not understand why this mattered. In the end, Hoover sent word to President Wilson about the critical famine in Europe, and Wilson determined that the American government would feed the starving people of Europe without anyone's permission. Food reached the liberated countries and the neutral lands quickly. But the European Allies kept American aid from Germany and Austria.

Hoover's men in Germany reported that the food shortage there was worse than before. Millions of waifs and orphans were already diseased and undernourished. Unless they could be helped quickly, those who survived would be a generation of incompetents and criminal brutes. Even then, many of them were beyond repair.

The European Allies said, "No food for Germany." Four months were lost before they came to an agreement to allow the Germans to be fed. Hoover started the food moving into the German harbors as soon as they were opened. But the months of starvation had created a hatred in the German nation that lasted a generation. The women and children had suffered too long and a mine had been planted that would blow up twenty years later.

ELEVEN

WHILE Hoover's men were getting the people fed and the railroads running, the houses rebuilt, and the hospitals working again, the Allies were wrangling over the peace treaty.

President Wilson had gone abroad with the United States mission to write the peace he had dreamed of: a peace that would end war, free the small nations, bring a new order; a peace that would bring the countries of the world together in a League of Nations. He had a great ideal of a lasting peace.

The European powers were not impressed with American ideals. Now that they had won the war, they wished to collect damages and inflict revenge for their losses. Their governments had already made treaties and agreements with each other about what each should gain from this victory and they did not intend to let the American President interfere with their plans.

President Wilson had come to the peace table with his Fourteen Points, the principles upon which he said the peace must rest. They had been his proclamation to the world of American ideals of peace. The Allied statesmen knew what they were. When Germany and Austria had asked for an armistice, it had been clearly understood that the Fourteen Points would be the basis for peace.

But by the time the statesmen sat down at the peace table, the plans of the European Allies for rearranging Europe were in direct conflict with the Fourteen Points. They were opposed to the American President throughout the negotiations, beginning with the question of feeding neutral and enemy civilians.

The European statesmen as well as the American President turned to Hoover for information and advice. His organization, working in more than twenty countries, kept him informed from day to day of the condition of the various peoples and of their hopes for the future. Hoover saw clearly that unless the defeated countries were allowed to develop free governments, to develop their economies, to provide jobs for their men, and to become self-supporting, the war would not be over. He was not concerned with revenge for past wrongs nor with punishment or advantage. He was concerned only with the making of a good peace. In the face of the prejudice and greed that he saw daily at the peace table, he became gloomy and pessimistic.

In April, President Wilson became ill. When he was back at work again, weakened by his illness, he was a changed man. He stopped fighting and gave in on one after another of his cherished Fourteen Points, hoping that by yielding so much he could at least keep the League of Nations. In the end he hardly realized how much he was conceding.

When the treaty was finally written early in May, Hoover studied it with a sense of doom: the terms written there would lead to misery and disaster. In spite of protest and argument from Hoover and from John Maynard Keynes—a young economist with the British delegation—and General Smuts—another British official, able and farseeing—who felt alike about it, the Great Powers signed the Treaty of Versailles on June 28, 1919. Hoover's fears began to be fulfilled within ten years.

It has been said since that of all the men who took part in World War I, in the Allied victory, and in the making of the peace of Versailles, Herbert Hoover was the only man who came out of that ordeal with an enhanced reputation. He knew the reasons for the European fears and demands. He said of the peace table: "The genes of a thousand years of inbred hate and fear of every generation were in their blood. Revenge for past wrongs rose every hour of the day. . . . Every warring nation in Europe was exhausted, economically desperate, and most of them hungry."

He could not blame hungry people for feeling desperate. What he tried to do for the peace of Versailles was to adjust the difference between victor and vanquished so that in the future no one need be hungry. What he knew, from his years of work with the European peoples and their governments, was that this adjustment was something America could never do for them. They must some day make their own peace.

Poland was one of the countries that had suffered most. Within two months of the armistice, in early January, 1919, Hoover sent a staff of his men to help Poland. They found almost total devastation. Armies had invaded and retreated seven times, destroying and destroying again. Hundreds of thousands of people had died of starvation. The cities were almost without food, and starving, swollen children crawled in the streets, digging in trash for scraps to eat.

The relief men set up soup kitchens and distribution centers and began feeding the people quickly. They found medical supplies. They brought in used and army-surplus clothing. They furnished the Poles with tons of raw cotton so their own mills could begin operating again, thereby making jobs as well as fabric. They helped the government begin trading with other countries. They found tools for the farmers, and crops were planted in the spring of 1919. Hoover's organization was a preview of UNRRA that came decades later.

Prime Minister Ignace Jan Paderewski, the great pianist and patriot had begged President Wilson to visit a grateful Poland before he went home to America. Wilson was unable to make the visit and he asked Herbert Hoover to represent him. Hoover took with him a delegation of generals and admirals to make the visit suitably impressive, and they arrived in Warsaw on August 12, 1919, seven months after the first food shipments had arrived.

The Poles wished to honor the American visit appropriately. And, although Hoover usually avoided cheers and adulation, in this case he accepted them as outpourings of gratitude for his country and his President.

110

The children of Warsaw gave Hoover the most cherished reception of his visit

In Warsaw, the children gave Hoover the reception he cherished more than any other during his visit. They came from the soup kitchens in trainloads, many in rags, carrying paper banners with American and Polish colors on them. They formed into a parade and romped past the American Friend, waving their tin cups and banners, cheering and gay. After seven months of American care, they had learned to laugh again.

The French minister broke down and left the reviewing stand. As he passed Hoover he said to him, "There has never been a review of honor in all history that I would prefer for myself, to that which has been given to you today." There were tears in Hoover's eyes, too, as he watched the healthy, happy children go by.

A startled rabbit leaped out of the grass and ran down the track. Whooping and squealing with joy, the children broke ranks and chased after it. When they caught the rabbit, they brought it to Mr. Hoover for a present.

They could not understand why he wept.

Hoover stayed on in Europe until September, winding up the affairs of the relief organization. During that time he continued the contribution to his country's knowledge that he had begun in 1914, when he had asked his CRB staff to collect the fugitive documents of the war.

Following that beginning, he had engaged professionals in the capitals of the warring nations to help in the collection. General Pershing—commander of the American Expeditionary Forces in Europe—had detached fifteen historians from the armed forces to collect documents. When governments collapsed, new governments gave their country's archives to the Americans, knowing they would be safe. Leaders who were overthrown gave their records to the Hoover collection. Hoover sent cargoes of this material back to America as ballast in the holds of the ships that had brought food to Europe. These cargoes went to Stanford University and were the nucleus of the Hoover War Library, known today as the Hoover Institution on War, Revolution and Peace.

After the armistice he brought a historian to Europe at his own expense and set up a fund of $50,000 to finance further work. Today, the Hoover Institution on War, Revolution and Peace holds the greatest collection of documents on these subjects in the world, and the collection continues to grow as history passes by.

Before he left Europe in September, Hoover made a final, personal inspection of the relief centers in the major countries. He wished to do this quietly and without notice. But the whole continent knew who had fed them when they were starving, and the people poured into the streets when they heard he was passing.

Cities in more than twenty countries gave his name to parks, squares, and streets. Dozens of cities struck Hoover medals. Warsaw set up his statue in one of the parks. Finland added a new word to its language: "hooveri," meaning benevolence. Letters of gratitude and affection poured in through the years, carrying four million signatures.

Belgium wanted to pay Hoover the public tribute of a royal order of nobility. This he brusquely refused.

He had always disliked European decorations and titles, feeling they had been too often used to beguile Americans into a false sentimentality. Still, he did not object to his men receiving them. Knowing that such decorations (he called them "buttons") meant a great deal to some of his hardworking loyal colleagues, he told the Belgian officials he would appreciate their honoring his staff.

But King Albert of Belgium found an honor that Hoover did not refuse. He created a new order with only one member: The Friend of Belgium and Honorary Citizen of Belgium. He requested Hoover to attend the special session of the Belgian Parliament to witness the unanimous passage of the bill confirming the new order. The designation "Friend of Belgium" was a rare tribute that Hoover was truly proud to have.

Part V

Secretary of Commerce

"I knew that if a man engaged in public life he was bound to create opposition every time he took a stand on a public question; that he was fated to accumulate enemies; that in the United States the laws of libel and slander had litttle potency, and that the customary form of reply to sober argument was proof of guilt by association or assumption of corrupt motives. It was the bitter experience of all public men from George Washington down that democracies are at least contemporarily fickle and heartless."

—Herbert Hoover, *Memoirs*

The Library of Louvain, in Belgium, rebuilt with American help after the destruction of World War I, and rebuilt again after World War II (see page 124)

TWELVE

WHEN Herbert Hoover sailed for America in September, 1919, he was disillusioned with Europe and he had only one aim: to go home to California and be with his family again. And he had only one hope: to return to private life and to practice engineering again, where he could work out constructive plans with reasonable men.

Upon his return he found himself a hero in America. This came to him as a jolt. Public acclaim embarrassed him. He never liked crowds and he disliked intensely the social contact with strangers expected of a hero.

When a man becomes a hero to the American people it is not easy to escape their attentions. While he was spending a month with "a great lady and two satisfactory boys" at home, hundreds of letters, cables, telegrams, and telephone calls intruded. Papers wanted statements; magazines wanted articles. It seemed as if everyone in the land wanted a speech. At last he gave out a statement parodying an engineering report:

"I plan to adhere to the following rules for one month:
"I will reply to no telephone calls, I am spending a month with two vigorous small boys. . . .
"I must decline the honor of speaking at sixty-four public meetings . . . I am satisfied that the American people will be gratified to find a citizen who wants to keep still . . .
"I offer this intimate disclosure of private affairs so it may be seen that I contemplate no mischief against this Commonwealth."

He had his month with his wife and sons, fishing and hiking

He had his month fishing and hiking and camping in the California mountains

and camping in the California mountains. His love of the wilderness life was reinforced now by the life he had left. Fishing had been his sport ever since Tad had shown him how to put a worm on a hook years before. From fishing he gained repose and that vital uplift he always found when he was in touch with nature.

He said, "Life is not comprised entirely of making a living or of arguing about the future or defaming the past. It is the break of waves in the sun, the contemplation of the eternal flow of the stream, the stretch of forest and mountain in their manifestation of the Maker—it is all these that soothe our troubles, shame our wickedness, and inspire us to esteem our fellow men—especially other fishermen."

When the month was over, all the problems were still waiting for him. The Senate was debating whether or not to accept the Versailles peace treaty. The American people and some of their senators were arguing about the League of Nations. Accounts and reports of the war relief organizations must be completed. Millions of waifs in Europe were still hungry and the Children's Relief must go on.

And he was still a popular figure.

Papers called him "a leading American." A London paper called him "the biggest man who has emerged on the Allied side during the war." The New York World said, "It is a place unique in history that Mr. Hooover has won. . . ." The New York Times had his name on their list of the ten most important living Americans.

Hoover read this acclaim skeptically. It sounded good but he knew from his experience in public service and from his knowledge of history that a man in public life met opposition as quickly as support. Some day he would be accused in these same papers of dishonesty, corruption, and stupidity. It had happened to all public men from George Washington down to President Wilson. Public life was an ordeal and Hoover wondered if five years were not enough to give to it. Perhaps the time had come when he could go back to his mining profession and his private life.

119

The Hoovers began building their dream house . . . It was planned for outdoor living, with terraces and gardens opening from the house

He opened offices in San Francisco and New York and staffed them. He and Mrs. Hoover began building their dream house from plans Mrs. Hoover had been working over for years. It was a Hopi house, with the flat roof and geometric masses of the homes of the Pueblo Indians in the Southwest. It was planned for outdoor living, with terraces and gardens, and was set atop a hill on the Stanford campus, facing the university, with magnificent views of the mountains and the San Francisco Bay.

While Mrs. Hoover was building their home, Mr. Hoover was continuing his work with Children's Relief. The American Relief Administration (ARA), which Hoover had set up in Paris while the armistice talks were delaying food for the hungry, would have to continue to feed and care for the health of many millions of children and adults in Europe for another year and more. Hoover now led drives to raise the money for that work.

His committee found one of the most effective means of raising funds to be the banquet for the "Invisible Guest." Many of these were held throughout the United States. In the center of the head table stood an empty high chair with a lighted candle on its tray. The guests were served the same kind of food that the ARA was serving to the undernourished children of Europe. Within three months, tens of millions of dollars came in to help feed the children of Europe.

In 1921 the Russians asked for help. Hoover's inquiries about the great famine in the Ukraine and in the Volga basin showed that, without help, from fifteen to twenty million people would die of starvation. Hoover demanded the cooperation of the Soviet government: American prisoners must be freed; American relief workers must be allowed to administer the relief and travel without interference throughout Russia; Americans must be permitted to organize local committees to help them; and Russia would have to provide free storage for supplies, free transportation, and office space, as well as Soviet gold to pay for food. The Soviet government agreed to these demands and, for almost two years, the ARA fed millions of undernourished children in Soviet Russia.

121

American Relief Association cares for the children of Vienna, during the famine following the war

"The Invisible Guest" at the head table between Herbert Hoover and General John Pershing at a New York banquet

Russian children wait for hours before mealtime so that they will not miss the food distributed by the ARA kitchen in Ufa, 1,000 miles east of Moscow, during the famine of 1921

A section of one of the many warehouses in Russia used for storage and distribution of American aid

In his letter of gratitude later, in 1923, Kamenev said:
". . . all the people inhabiting the Union of Soviet Socialist Republics never will forget the aid rendered to them by the American people . . . holding it to be a pledge of the future friendship of the two nations."

Hoover was also concerned with the needs of American children. Thirty percent of the draftees in the World War had been rejected, and this revealed serious defects in health and education. He became president of the American Child Health Association which was working for health inspection in schools, more compulsory education, and prohibition of child labor. Hoover worked from that time on for a constitutional amendment to stop the long hours of hard labor for children. The amendment did not pass, but the work of the Child Health Association brought about, in many states, better laws about children's welfare.

The time had come to wind up the affairs of the Committee for Relief in Belgium. The CRB had finished its work with $34,000,000 left over. This surplus was due to the careful management of the women of Belgium and belonged to the government of Belgium. The government asked Hoover to use the money as he wished for the benefit of their people.

He gave $7,000,000 to a foundation for the improvement of education in Belgium. He distributed $18,000,000 among universities and technical schools there. He set up a CRB educational foundation in New York, whose purpose was Belgian-American student exchange. The money that was left rebuilt the Library of of Louvain and the University of Brussels.

While he was completing the work of the agencies and his activities of the war years, Hoover was observing life in his own land. He was convinced, after twenty years of work in foreign lands, that here in America the people had developed a system that promised and delivered more than that of any other land. He had been thinking about the American system during the European years, and now he was ready to make a comment upon it.

He wrote a small book called *American Individualism* which

124

recorded his belief in the American way and his understanding of the special qualities that made it unique. He believed that individualism had created democracy and that only through democracy could individuals rise. He believed that the function of government was to cure abuses, to prevent individuals and groups from interfering with each other's liberties, and to regulate the conduct of business and public affairs so each individual would benefit. Individual freedom and progress required individual responsibility for the welfare of other individuals, for the social force that built America sprang from the chance and the stimulation of each individual to develop his own heart, mind, and ability to its highest potential. He said that the higher purposes of individualism must find their support in things of the spirit. He was as much concerned with the spirit of America as with her material welfare.

The spirit of America in 1920 was weary.

Workers had been striking since the armistice for better hours and higher wages. Over four million workers were involved in more than twenty-five hundred strikes, and it seemed as if the war won in Europe had sprung up in new form at home. A "Red" scare flamed across the country as people blamed Communists for unrest. Racial troubles broke out and flared into wholesale violence, with lynchings and burnings in the South and the worst race riots in American history up to that time. And the battle over the League of Nations went on at a feverish emotional pitch—tempers ran high and accusations were brutal.

The country was tired of high purpose and was ready to go back to the golden days before the war. In the election of 1920 they rejected Woodrow Wilson's party and the League, and elected Warren G. Harding to the Presidency. He had talked about returning to "normalcy" and that was what the people wanted.

Soon after the election Mr. Harding told Herbert Hoover he would like to have him in the cabinet, either as Secretary of the Interior or as Secretary of Commerce. Before Hoover decided about this, Daniel Guggenheim came to see him.

The Guggenheim brothers had the greatest mining company in the world. They wanted Hoover to join them as a partner, and they offered him a salary reported to be a guaranteed minimum of $500,000 a year. In the Guggenheim empire he would have become enormously wealthy.

But Hoover had come back from Europe with new and deeper insights into the needs of his country, and he had ideas about what he would like to do for America. He spent a week considering the choice between private fortune with personal freedom and public service where he would be a target for enemies and criticism. Once, long ago, he had said he wanted to get into the Big Game sometime. Now he made his choice, and no one but his wife then knew about the fortune he put aside when he accepted the offer to become the Secretary of Commerce under President Harding. He chose the Commerce post because there he thought he could carry out some of the convictions he had presented in *American Individualism*.

Hoover believed that the greatest personal happiness flowed from personal achievement. For this men needed jobs. Without the freedom to work as one chose and use one's money as one liked, intellectual and spiritual freedom died. More than that, he knew the hungry and downtrodden people of Europe looked to free America as their golden hope. For him there was no more important job to be done than to keep America the hope of the world.

He hoped also to lift the eyes of America to a greater spiritual goal, "a lifting purpose greater than the struggle for materialism . . . a higher pitch of economic life, a finer regard for the rights of others, a stronger devotion to the obligations of citizenship." The American Friend believed that spiritual growth could develop more easily when the fear of poverty was lifted from man's spirit.

He saw in the Commerce Department a chance to remove that fear of poverty, and he brought to the post a program that expanded the department far beyond anything it had ever been before. He thought the department could contribute something to every aspect of the nation's economic life: labor, management, business and

126

industry; mines, water resources, conservation of forests and public lands; aeronautics, radio, electric power and railways; agricultural marketing, foreign trade, banking, housing, child welfare.

To accomplish all this, he demanded a voice in the policies of labor, agriculture, finance, foreign affairs, and in all the important economic decisions of President Harding's administration, if he were to accept the post of Secretary of Commerce. He specified that the secretaries of the departments of Agriculture, Interior, State, and Labor should understand this. The President agreed.

Thus launched in political life and striding so aggressively to the forefront of the Administration, Hoover began to collect enemies. Some of them he had collected earlier. The powerful progressive senators of the Republican party, William E. Borah of Idaho, Hiram W. Johnson of California, and George W. Norris of Nebraska, had resented bitterly Hoover's support of President Wilson's League of Nations and his work to elect congressmen in 1918 who would support Wilson, some of whom were Democrats.

Reactionary Republican senators also opposed him, and two of them—Boies Penrose of Pennsylvania and Henry Cabot Lodge, Sr., of Massachusetts—held up his appointment to the Commerce post for three months, until President Harding told them he would give them Andrew Mellon, whom they wanted as Secretary of the Treasury, only if they accepted Hoover.

Hoover knew who his enemies were and made little effort to conciliate them, since conciliation would have meant compromise. When Hoover considered he was right about a question, he would try to persuade others to see it his way, but he would neither compromise nor trade his conviction for votes. However, he was not worried about the opposition. He might be the least-liked public servant by the professional politicians, but in the twenties he was the most popular administrator among the people of the country.

His first step in his new office was to reorganize the Commerce Department, removing untrained political appointees and bringing in men of technical training who qualified through Civil Service.

He hired two secretaries and three assistants for his own office, at his own expense, using his official pay for their salaries and making up the difference out of his own pocket. One of those assistants was Christian Herter, who rose in government service to become Secretary of State under President Eisenhower.

When Hoover entered President Harding's cabinet in the spring of 1921, the country was in a postwar depression. Five million men were out of work and President Harding called a conference on unemployment and appointed the Secretary of Commerce to direct it.

There had been depressions before. The normal business cycle was "boom and bust." The federal government had always assumed the cycle was inevitable and that business could recover from depressions by itself without government attention.

Hoover believed that government could do something about a sick economy. He called in leaders of industry, labor, banking, and agriculture, and asked employers to share the jobs and keep the wages high. He talked with governors of states about making more jobs in public construction, building highways and public buildings at once. The results showed quickly; increased employment meant increased buying, production started up again, and the depression was over within a year. The conference went on to collect unemployment statistics for use in fighting future slumps.

Early in 1922, the Secretary of Commerce determined to do something about the barbaric working conditions in the steel industry. In spite of the strikes of the past two years, men in steel were still working twelve hours a day, seven days a week, for a wage of twenty-eight dollars a week. Hoover directed the department to investigate the situation and, when he had the facts, the Secretary persuaded President Harding to call a dinner conference of steel manufacturers at the White House.

There, the Secretary of Commerce showed the executives his figures proving that the output per man was more profitable in the eight-hour-a-day, six-day week than in the eighty-four-hour week. The manufacturers were not convinced and protested that it was impossible to pay the same wages for forty-eight hours of work as for eighty-four. The debate grew bitter and the President ended the conference by asking the steel chiefs to set up a committee to make their own investigation and bring in a report.

Hoover left the dinner angry and discouraged. Reporters waiting on the porch of the White House wanted to know what the conference was about. He told them the President was trying to persuade the steel industry to go to the eight-hour shift and a forty-eight-hour week. This was big news and the papers headlined the story. The public responded with anticipation and hope.

When the steel committee sent in their report a year later, they promised nothing and asked for more time. Hoover drafted a letter for the President to sign, expressing keen disappointment, and gave it to the press. The public was so outraged that the steel companies backed down and adopted the forty-eight-hour week within a month. This was one of the few significant accomplishments of President Harding's Administration.

For Secretary Hoover, a major satisfaction was the fact that the victory had been gained through public protest, without requiring legislation. He said, "When abuses are cured by live individual conscience, by voluntary standards, then is the growth of moral perception fertilized in every individual character."

He was deeply conscious every day of the delicate line between government power and private enterprise. The dangers of government doing too much or doing too little were equally great. He disliked making changes by a show of power and he worked always to get the cooperation of people and business by offering the kind of guidance, information, and service they could use.

In developing foreign markets for American products, he consulted the leaders and officers in industry and trades about their needs, obstacles, and methods of selling. He set up commodity divisions within the department and asked various companies to name their own representatives whom he appointed as directors of the divisions. They collected facts and information for their own fields. Businessmen could find out by writing to the Department of Commerce about competition for their product, prices abroad, banking systems in various countries, and anything else that might be useful in approaching a new market. This concept of the Bureau of Foreign and Domestic Commerce was original with Secretary Hoover, and a major contribution to the growing business of the United States in the twenties.

The other major contribution in the Commerce post was his work in the elimination of industrial waste, which resulted in major economies in production, which in turn meant lower costs to the buyers. By industrial waste, he meant time-wasting strikes; the waste of manpower and money in unemployment; the recurring cycles of booms and slumps; the waste of money and motion in careless planning; time lost in transportation inefficiency; and a dozen other industrial habits and weaknesses. "Imperfect coordination," he called it.

He called together representatives of special departments of industry to help him decide where to start. After that meeting, a committee was appointed to cooperate with the Commerce Department in solving the problem. One of their earliest efforts was to standardize and simplify sizes and styles of thousands of items. For example, there were sixty-six sizes of paving bricks being made and marketed; seventy-four combinations of lengths and widths in bed sizes; dozens of unnecessary sizes in lumber; every combination of nuts and bolts had different thread sizes. Manufacturers were making too many sizes and kinds of everything. In working on this problem, Hoover called upon the Standards Committee of the Engineering Societies which cooperated constantly with the department.

The Department of Commerce offered information to industry about the problem and ideas for its solution, inviting any company who was interested to ask for their "simplified practice." When the brick manufacturers asked about the service, Hoover invited representative men from the industry, and also from the consumers— the city governments who bought paving bricks—to meet together. Fairly quickly, they agreed to reduce sixty-six sizes to eleven sizes.

Eventually they went further and brought the choice down to five.

As industry began to understand the savings involved in setting standards that would apply throughout the industry, one after another appealed to the Commerce Department to advise them. Standard sizes were adopted for sizes of paper; automobile tires; nuts and bolts for industry; plumbing; window frames; and many other items.

In 1925, Mark Sullivan reported the success of the program for standardizing the products of American industry: American business was saving half a billion dollars a year through this transformation accomplished by the Commerce Department, while all the gold taken from the Klondike in seven years had totaled less than a hundred million dollars. This was Hoover's contribution to American business, which has become a permanent working process, and has been responsible for a large part of America's tremendous technical advances since the twenties.

Water conservation was an important part of the program for cutting out waste, and Hoover developed seven major projects for navigation, irrigation for dry lands, electrical power, and flood control. Of these, the Colorado River Dam at Boulder Canyon was of first importance. This dam was planned to give water for the irrigation of seven western states in which water was the scarcest and most precious resource. Each state was afraid that what one gained another might lose, and they had been wrangling over the Boulder Canyon Dam since the beginning of the century.

Hoover spent months in conference with the state committees. At last he found a formula that all states would accept. The compact for the Boulder Canyon Dam was signed, for sentimental reasons, at Hoover's suggestion, in the three-hundred-year-old Governor's Palace at Santa Fe, New Mexico. After twenty years, the dam was on its way.

Opposition from legislatures and engineers delayed the building of the dam for another eight years. It was 1930 before the work could actually begin. This dam was Hoover's special project and he worked on some of the engineering himself.

131

In his overall program for the river systems, he outlined the St. Lawrence Waterway from the Atlantic to the Great Lakes. In 1924, the President appointed Hoover chairman of a commission to discuss the project with the Canadian commission. While progress in this planning was very slow, Hoover's efforts in the years between 1922 and 1932 led eventually to the great St. Lawrence Seaway which opened to traffic in 1959, dedicated by President Eisenhower and Queen Elizabeth II.

THIRTEEN

IN 1923, President Harding died. Calvin Coolidge became president, and Hoover continued as Secretary of Commerce under him.

The years in the Commerce Department were among the most satisfying in Hoover's long life. Mrs. Hoover found a pleasant colonial house with an acre of garden in Washington and again made a home away from California. She had a gift for making a welcoming and comfortable home with its own personality in all the corners of the world, and her husband admired this gift highly.

The boys were growing up now. Herbert entered Stanford University the year his father was sworn into the cabinet. Allan was fifteen and attending a public high school in Washington. His father believed public schools were the best introduction to American life.

Allan was attached to pets. He had two dogs and two cats and two ducks. The ducks he trained to sit on the front porch, and passersby laughed when they saw them. He had turtles he had found in the woods. He had two small alligators, which had to sleep in the bathtub at night. His father approved of pets and enjoyed Allan's activities. Watching his boys grow up was one of Hoover's deepest pleasures. He wrote to a young correspondent who asked about his family: "We have in our family 2 small Boys, 2 Cats, 11 Goldfish, 1 Canary, 3 Frogs, 14 Chickens, 2 Turtles, 1 Rabbit. . . . We also have 1,000,000 mosquitos."

The family was surrounded with friends. Hardly a meal went by without guests. Visitors came from all over the country, from Europe and Asia. They stayed as houseguests, or at the least for a meal—often breakfast. Washington friends joined the Hoovers

The living room of the Hoover house in Palo Alto

Mr. Hoover went deep-sea fishing in Florida for a week each winter

for Sunday night suppers almost every weekend. Some of their closest friends were the Harlan F. Stones and the Mark Sullivans. Harlan Stone was the Attorney General and Mark Sullivan was a distinguished journalist.

The eight years of cabinet service went by in the first unbroken term of family life the Hoovers had known. They spent time in Palo Alto each summer. Mr. Hoover went deep-sea fishing for a week in Florida each winter. Otherwise they were together in Washington. Allan finished high school in 1925 and entered Stanford. Young Herbert graduated that same year from Stanford and announced he was going to get married. And suddenly the family years were almost gone.

Outside the family, Mrs. Hoover was devoting her attention to the Girl Scouts of America, a struggling organization then of fewer than a hundred thousand girls. She worked with them all the years she was in Washington. She was elected president and raised over two million dollars for the organization. Under her leadership the membership grew to nearly a million girls.

Mrs. Hoover worked with the Girl Scouts while she was in Washington

In 1927, the country was stirred to wild excitement by the flight of Charles A. Lindbergh from New York to Paris. Eight years earlier, a New York man had offered a prize of $25,000 for the first nonstop flight between New York and Paris. None had tried to win it. But in 1927, three planes waited for fair weather at Roosevelt Field, New York, to try the first nonstop flight across the Atlantic.

Two of them had crews of two or more. Lindbergh had flown the *Spirit of St. Louis* in from the Pacific Coast alone and proposed to fly the Atlantic alone. Reporters called him "Lucky Lindy" and "Flying Fool."

On May 20 he decided that the weather was good enough for him. He had his plane fueled, and before eight in the morning he took off alone. The wires flashed the word across the country

Charles A. Lindbergh received the Congressional Medal of Honor for his achievement, but not until August, 1930, when it was presented to him by President Hoover. In this picture, from left to right, center front: Mrs. Hoover, Lindbergh, the President, Mrs. Lindbergh

that Lindbergh had started for Paris, and the whole country focused their hopes on his flight, following him hour by hour.

The wires reported the next day that he had reached the coast of Ireland, that he was crossing England, that he was over the Channel. The long hours went by and the American people followed every hour and every mile. When the news came through that he had landed safely at Le Bourget airfield near Paris, after thirty-three and a half hours of solo flight, the country went wild with joy. Lindbergh was the greatest national hero of his time.

After that historic flight, commercial aviation began to develop rapidly, and the Secretary of Commerce directed the development of airways, airports, research laboratories in plane construction. By 1929, American commercial aviation was flying over 25 million miles a year.

In the spring of 1927, also, one of the greatest floods in history broke the banks and levees of the Mississippi River. Water covered areas as wide as a hundred and fifty miles in places all the way from Cairo, Illinois, to the Gulf of Mexico, as the crest traveled a thousand miles downstream in two months. A million and a half people were driven from their homes, two million acres of crops, thousands of cattle, and hundreds of millions of dollars in buildings and community property were destroyed.

As the flood broke, the governors of the six states along the river asked for Herbert Hoover in this emergency, and President Coolidge sent him to Memphis to mobilize state and local authorities and militia, army engineers, Coast Guard, weather bureaus, and Red Cross.

He got sawmills located along the length of the river to make a thousand rough boats in ten days and rented outboard motors for power, to move people out of the flooded areas. His organization established tent towns on high ground, put in sewers, electric lights, kitchens, feeding halls, and hospitals. The people moved were small farmers and villagers, white and Negro. They were so well cared for, fed, and entertained, that for many of them it was the first real holiday they had ever known.

When the flood subsided, Hoover saw a great chance to improve the general health of the people in the southern states along the Mississippi. With a gift from the Rockefeller Foundation, he set up health units—a doctor, trained nurse, and sanitary engineer—to work for a year in each of the hundred flooded counties. Within the year they had stamped out malaria, pellagra, and typhoid from those counties: a permanent gain from the flood disaster.

Another gain from the flood for Hoover was his discovery that Americans had the ability to organize themselves in emergency. In Europe it had been hard to find local leadership. In the Mississippi counties the least suggestion brought out efficient organization. He believed the reason for this special ability lay in the individualism and freedom of the American system: it had bred a different kind of people.

Following the flood disaster, Hoover drew up a plan for flood control of the Mississippi, which was carried out during the next five years. The lower Mississippi has never flooded since that time, in spite of a major flood coming down the Ohio ten years later, and massive floods from the Twin Cities to Hannibal, Mo., in 1965.

With all the satisfactions Hoover found in the office of the Secretary of Commerce, there were disappointments too.

The farmers of the country were in a "depression," after 1920. They had learned how to produce in abundance for the needs of a hungry world; after the war, when so much food was no longer needed, the markets were glutted with more food than could be sold. Prices went down, and the lower the prices, the more the farmers raised, hoping to sell more to make up for the price drop. When prices rose, the farmers raised more again, hoping to make up for the poor years. Hoover had been concerned with the special problems of the farmers ever since 1917, when he had worked with them as Food Administrator.

Now, as Secretary of Commerce, he insisted on making the marketing of farm production the business of his department. The Department of Agriculture, he said, should confine itself to the production end. The Secretary of Agriculture, Henry A. Wallace, bitterly protested this invasion of his department. He claimed that the Department of Agriculture should manage every aspect of the farmers' welfare.

Hoover went ahead with his plans for solving surplus and marketing problems of agriculture while Secretary Wallace developed his own plans. Hoover worked out better cooperation among railways, farm organizations, and city markets, to save millions of dollars of marketing costs. He supported the farmers' cooperative movement—their own organizations for the solving of marketing problems.

Wallace worked out a plan to sell the surplus farm products at a fixed price. The government, according to his plan, would buy surplus at this fixed price, and sell it abroad for any price they could get—the world price, which was lower than the American price. This is "dumping," and foreign nations resent it because it interferes with the sales of their own agricultural products. The losses from dumping would be made up by a tax upon the farmers, according to the quantity of surplus each farmer sold. This tax was called "an equalization fee," and it was designed to discourage surpluses.

Hoover believed the guaranteed price would encourage surpluses and he disapproved of any form of price-fixing. He proposed that the farmers should be paid for taking marginal lands out of production, as the government had paid manufacturers to reduce over-expanded plants after the war. This "marginal lands" program the Agriculture department refused to consider.

Wallace had never liked Hoover. He had criticized the Food Administration during the war, and now he was bitter because a man he disliked was managing affairs of the farmers that Wallace believed should be managed by his own department. The struggle between the two secretaries created partisan support in the Congress, and the progressive senators formed the Farm Bloc, under the leadership of Borah of Idaho, Johnson of California, Robert La Follette of Wisconsin, Arthur Capper of Kansas, and George

Secretary of Commerce Hoover and
President Calvin Coolidge

Norris of Nebraska, among others. The Farm Bloc supported the Secretary of Agriculture. But President Coolidge supported the Secretary of Commerce. In this impasse, the farmers went on producing too large a quantity on too much acreage.

It was a problem that would go on for decades. Neither the farmers themselves nor the experts could agree on the best solution. For thirty years, no Administration, trying one answer after another, was able to solve the farm problem.

Another disappointment for Hoover as Secretary of Commerce was his failure to achieve improvements in the operation of the federal government itself. He had seen, during his service as Food Administrator, the great waste in the operation of the government: agencies duplicated each other's work; red tape slowed communications between departments and delayed decisions, wasting hours of time; heads of little bureaus made themselves important by tyrannizing over their little domains, clogging the wheels of government.

Hoover had hoped to correct some of this inefficiency, and he proposed to put all the agencies with the same general purpose under the same administrative supervision; to separate advisory functions from administrative ones; and to relieve the President of some of the unnecessary detail of his office. But too many politicians had something to gain by keeping things running the way they were, and President Coolidge preferred to let things alone whenever possible. The Secretary of Commerce could get no action from either the President or Congress on his proposals for executive reorganization.

Another worry for the Secretary of Commerce was the prosperity cycle the country was enjoying after 1925. By 1927, business was having the most exciting boom it had ever had. Hoover had been working since 1922 to temper the "boom periods" of business in order to avoid the depressions that always followed. But businessmen were confident that this great prosperity in the late twenties could never end and President Coolidge refused to experiment with anything that might check the boom.

When Hoover warned about speculation, gambling, and possible losses in the jumping stock market, speculators and economists called him a spoilsport. Even the working folk were too prosperous in 1927 to listen to warnings, and the businessmen, who were too busy making money to look beyond the present prosperity, laughed at him—or they resented his "radicalism."

141

At the close of his term of office in 1928, Hoover summed up the economic progress in eight years as "due to the power of a free people." Working hours had gone down and wages had increased. Electrical power had doubled. The population had risen eight percent but national income had increased forty-five percent. People had acquired telephones, radios, and fourteen million automobiles. Sixty-six percent more children were now in high school than before, seventy-five percent more in college.

"One of the oldest and perhaps the noblest of human aspirations," he said, "has been the abolition of poverty. We in America today are nearer to the final triumph over poverty than ever before."

But he hoped for greater things for his country than prosperity alone. He said, "Economic advancement is not an end in itself . . . Integrity, generosity, cultivation of mind, willingness to sacrifice, spaciousness of spirit—these are the qualities whereby we, growing bigger and richer and more powerful, may fulfill the promise of America."

142

Part VI

President of the United States

"The President is not only the leader of a party, he is the President of the whole people. He must interpret the conscience of America. He must guide his conduct by the idealism of our people. The Presidency is no dictatorship. It is not intended to be. Safeguards are provided to prevent it. Our fathers knew that men were not made for government, but government for men—to aid and to serve them. Our government rests solely upon the will of the people; it springs from the people."

—Herbert Hoover
(Quoted in *Hoover Off the Record* by Theodore G. Joslin)

The desk and chair used by President Hoover in the White House

FOURTEEN

IN AUGUST, 1927, President Coolidge announced that he did not choose to run for reelection in 1928. As soon as the President's statement appeared, letters and telegrams poured in to Mr. Hoover, asking him to run for the Presidency.

Some Republican leaders hoped that Mr. Coolidge would change his mind; they did not want Hoover for their candidate. The "Old Guard" and progressive Republican senators did not want him. Most of them had hated Hoover ever since he had supported President Wilson in 1918. They knew he would not play the game their way, trading votes. And they distrusted those friends of Hoover who were working with him. They were not politicians either. Politicians they could count on. With amateurs they would not know what to expect.

Money and banking men in New York did not want Hoover. He had been trying to stop the boom. Farmers did not want him: he had not solved the farm problem. Nobody wanted Hoover but the people.

Between spring and the Republican Convention in June, 1928, some seven hundred friends of Hoover built an organization to gain primary votes and convention delegates for him. Small businessmen were for him. Miners, railway workers, union men, and nonunion men were for him. Women's clubs and social workers were for him. Stanford people, from President Ray Lyman Wilbur down to the students, were for him. Everyone who had ever worked for his relief organizations and the Food Administration was for him. When the convention balloted for the Presidential nomination, Hoover won on the first ballot.

The Democrats that year nominated Alfred E. Smith, the

first Catholic ever to run for the Presidency. He had been a New York politician for twenty years or more and governor of New York for eight years, with an excellent record. His name was put in nomination by Franklin D. Roosevelt.

Al Smith was a genial mixer and a back-slapper. He loved people and crowds and excitement. He campaigned in a brown derby hat with a big cigar and drew large, enthusiastic crowds. But bigotry and whispered prejudice entered the campaign almost at once. People raised alarms about the danger of a Catholic in the Presidency: he would let the Pope tell him what to do. Some whispered that the Smiths were too crude socially for the White House.

Hoover resented the unfair personal and religious attacks on Al Smith. Al Smith resented the personal attacks on Hoover from some of the progressive enemies in his own party. Both men carried on campaigns about issues, with no personal hostility, and both retained a friendly regard for each other afterward.

Hoover told the people his program for the country and his philosophy of government. He was a liberal, and his liberalism meant political equality for all men, free speech, free assembly, free press, and the equality of economic justice and opportunity. He believed that more power for the government led to less freedom for individuals. Government conduct of business, he said, would destroy political equality, increase abuse and corruption, and undermine the development of leadership. But government was responsible for regulating business in such a way that one group of citizens did not deprive another group of its rightful freedoms and equality. Here again, he was pointing out to the people the delicate balance between government control and free enterprise.

He talked, too, about the economic leadership the Republican Administration had shown during his years as Secretary of Commerce, and claimed for the GOP all the credit for the prosperity of the past years.

On many of the issues Hoover and Al Smith were in accord: the reforms in child welfare, in business practice, in the prison system; the better organization of the federal government; the development of water resources and oil conservation.

They differed on the farm program. Governor Smith favored the McNary-Haugen bill, which would fix prices for produce and dump surplus abroad. Hoover said this would mean government control for the farmer's production and distribution.

And they differed on Prohibition.

The prohibition of alcoholic beverages had been written into the Constitution nine years before at the crest of the reforming zeal of the years before the war. During that time it had seemed like a needed reform. But following the war, in the twenties, people who wanted to drink liquor began to show that no law was going to stop them. They bought liquor from smugglers, and quickly criminals found that "bootlegging" whiskey brought them a great deal of money. By 1928, crime had become organized by gangsters because of Prohibition, and people were arguing as to whether or not Prohibition had been a mistake.

Al Smith campaigned for repeal of the Prohibition amendment. Hoover refused to argue about it. He had never believed the Constitution was the proper place for such a law. But once the amendment had been adopted, he considered that it was the obligation of the President to uphold the Constitution, not to argue with it.

Hoover opened his campaign at Stanford University on August 11, 1928, the day after his fifty-fourth birthday. He gave his second address at West Branch, Iowa, on August 21.

There, old friends, who had known him in his childhood, organized to honor the hometown boy who was running for President of the United States. Boys who had slid down Cook's Hill with the candidate fifty years before sent letters and telegrams from London, Western Canada, Montana. The Hoovers found Mollie Brown, who was now Mrs. Carran, and kept her with them for breakfast at the cottage of his birth and on the platform during the afternoon program.

The remainder of the campaign Hoover found very arduous. He wrote his own speeches, never using a ghost writer then or

147

Mr. and Mrs. Hoover, with sons Herbert and Allan, at the Hoover birthplace in West Branch, Iowa, during the 1928 Presidential campaign

later, and each one took two to three weeks to compose and write to his own satisfaction.

He was never at his best before a crowd. Speaking was an ordeal for him, and before a big audience he sounded stiff and monotonous, reading to them rather than talking with them. He was always shy with strangers, and he could not open up with a crowd of several thousand strangers and act gay and witty as if he loved them all. Much later he admitted to a friend that he was scared to death at the opening of every speech.

However, in 1928 this was not important. He was still a hero to the American people, and they hardly noticed a coldness in his public personality. Probably, listening to him, they felt that he was only stiff and shy as they themselves would have been in his place.

It quickly developed into a dirty campaign and lies were thrown around freely by both Republicans and Democrats about each other's candidate. This kind of campaigning was disillusioning to both men, who respected each other highly then and afterward. Hoover was elected by one of the biggest majorities in the history of the Republican party His Vice President was Charles Curtis.

In the four months between his election and his inauguration the following March, the President-elect would have to find the men he wanted to work with him and outline the major programs of his administration. Hoover also decided to visit Latin America during this interim.

He had found, as Secretary of Commerce, that the United States was highly unpopular with her Latin American neighbors. Three earlier Presidents had sent American troops into Santo Domingo, Nicaragua, and Haiti to keep the peace. Hoover felt that better relations between the United States and Latin America were vitally important.

Mrs. Hoover went with him, sometimes speaking for him in Spanish. He took along an interpreter, a diplomatic staff, and twenty outstanding journalists (among them Will Irwin and Mark Sullivan), not only to show his recognition of the importance of the visit, but because he felt the experience would be valuable for the newsmen who could educate the people of the United States in Latin American relations.

He visited with the leaders of each country. He talked about cooperation between countries. He announced that during his Administration all American troops would be withdrawn from Latin American countries. And he stressed again and again the theme of "good neighbors" between neighboring countries. In this trip before his inauguration he laid the foundation of the Good Neighbor Policy between the United States and Latin America.

Upon his return to Washington he began to collect his cabinet. He wished to represent all parts of the country with men of ability. Frank B. Kellogg would serve as Secretary of State until June, to be followed by Henry L. Stimson of New York. The Attorney General was William D. Mitchell of Minnesota; Secretary of the Treasury, Andrew Mellon of Pennsylvania, who had served under Harding and Coolidge in that post; Secretary of War, James W. Good of Iowa; Secretary of the Navy, Charles Francis Adams of Massachusetts; Postmaster General, Walter F. Brown of Ohio; Secretary of Agriculture, Arthur M. Hyde of Missouri; Secretary of the Interior, Ray Lyman Wilbur, at that time president of Stanford University; Secretary of Commerce, Robert P. Lamont of Illinois; and Secretary of Labor, James J. Davis of Pennsylvania. They were all excellent public servants, and none of them was a politician. The Republican party resented that.

There were lists of other secretaries and general staff members, and later Hoover recorded his admiration for all the people who had served with him. No President, he said, was ever surrounded by men and women with more personal loyalty and devotion to public service. They did not always agree with him. But they could discuss their differences without publicity and without bitterness.

On a March day that was blustering, cold, and rainy, Herbert Clark Hoover took his oath of office as the thirty-first President of the United States. From West Branch, Iowa, two hundred

*Mrs. Mollie Brown Carran, who had been
Hoover's favorite teacher*

and seventy-five friends came to see their President inaugurated.

Among them were Mollie Brown Carran and her husband.
Hoover had always treated Mrs. Carran as a favorite member of
his family, and on Inauguration Day he invited her to sit near

Cartoon by Jay Darling on Hoover's inauguration

him on the platform for the ceremonies. During the reception that followed he asked Mrs. Carran to stay with them and introduce the Iowa party. Afterwards the Carrans were invited to lunch at the White House. Mrs. Carran sat on the President's right.

Hoover came into the White House at the very peak of his fame and popularity. He was regarded by the leaders of Europe as one of the greatest men in the world. He brought to the Presidency a wider range of interests, information, and experience than any President before him. He knew from his work as Secretary

152

of Commerce the social and business reforms the country needed, and he had a great program for bringing a better life to all the people of his country, and a vision for building peace in the world through international cooperation. A Washington newswoman reported that he was never so animated and assured as when he discussed his plans for world trade and peace during the first weeks of his Administration.

While he said nothing about his personal sense of service, he banked his Presidential salary in a special account and gave it entirely to charity, or to raise the wages of aides who could not otherwise work for him. This was a gesture of generosity unseen since the Administration of George Washington. From the day he undertook to organize the Belgian Relief in 1914, until his death fifty years later, Hoover never accepted for his private use any payment for any public service.

So he took on his new office with eager and vigorous anticipation. All the rest of his busy life had been preparation for this moment when Herbert Hoover could make his greatest contribution to his own country.

Hoover's Inaugural Medallion

The Hoovers moved again, this time from the pleasant house on S Street, where the ducks on the porch had watched the people, to the White House, where the people watched the President. For Hoover, the rooms and halls of the historic mansion were filled with the presence of the great leaders who had lived there before. The spirits of all the Presidents since John Adams surrounded him, and he felt their call to devotion for service to his country.

Of all the former Presidents, Abraham Lincoln had been Hoover's idol, and Hoover felt his presence there continually. He chose to work in the Lincoln study, and he restored it from its use as a bedroom in the days of Theodore Roosevelt to its original purpose with its original furnishings.

Over the mantel of the white marble fireplace he hung a large steel engraving of Lincoln and his cabinet which he had carried with him in his travels over the world. He and Mrs. Hoover hunted every garret and basement storage room to find the chairs that had belonged in the study. Four of the chairs in the engraving were found. The original desk was brought back to the study. On that desk, made from the timbers of the ship *Resolute*, Lincoln had signed the Emancipation Proclamation. It became Hoover's own work desk.

Looking from the windows facing south, Hoover could see the Washington Monument and the hills of Arlington. In the Lincoln study, he could feel the continuing pulse of history that had carried each President to success or failure, to honor or defeat.

Mrs. Hoover brought in their own furniture for the upstairs family rooms and made a "California room" at the west end of the long hall, with palms and bamboo furniture and grass rugs. A huge birdcage shaped like a fan was filled with songbirds. She arranged a corner of doll furniture to amuse small guests. And she became acquainted with the staff of servants who had served the White House before. The cook told her frankly that she had voted for Governor Smith. Mrs. Hoover assured her that the President did not care about her politics, but he did care about her cooking. Since the cooking was superb, she stayed at the White House until the Democratic President came in after the Hoovers.

Mrs. Hoover at the Monroe desk in the Red Room

Mrs. Hoover made the history of the White House her special project. She hired a friend to research through early records and write a history of the furnishings, and she herself continued hunting for original pieces that had become displaced through the years. One of her most exciting finds was a small mirror that a British soldier had looted from the White House in 1814. This she hung on the wall of the President's study. She was determined to restore the Red Room, which had been furnished originally by President Monroe in 1818 with furniture from France. This furniture had disappeared, but Mrs. Hoover found a fine craftsman who duplicated it. When Mrs. Hoover left the White House, she left the furniture as her gift to the nation.

To provide for some recreation and solitude, and to get away from Washington's summer heat, the Hoovers bought land for a

One of the log cabins at Rapidan

vacation spot on the Rapidan in the Blue Ridge Mountains, a hundred miles from the White House. There Mrs. Hoover built and furnished a family lodge with a direct telephone line to the White House, and log cabins for twelve to fifteen guests, whom they often took with them for weekends away from the White House.

Friends were essential to Hoover, and among them he was talkative, humorous, genial, and sympathetic. But he could not put on that face with strangers. Those who did not know him well thought him cold and indifferent. Part of this came from his deep shyness. Part of it was his concentration on the tasks in hand. Some have said he was too sensitive to criticism and this made him seem withdrawn. Some thought he was only the unemotional engineer. His friends disagreed with all these views. They knew

156

Interior of Rapidan cottage. Mrs. Hoover is knitting

that he craved affection, loved congenial company, and surrounded himself with close friends most of the time. He suffered under criticism, but he was too sane and philosophical to brood about it.

Whatever the reasons for his shyness and the diffidence that kept the crowd at a distance, Herbert Hoover came into the Presidency with great dreams for his country, with a high spiritual goal for his people, with a great reputation in the eyes of the world, and with a respect for the office that few Presidents have matched. And he brought to the office a temperament that would make the Presidency the toughest job he had ever undertaken.

It was the first elective office he had ever run for, and perhaps that, too, was part of the trouble. Because trouble started soon after his inauguration and snowballed terribly as the years went by.

FIFTEEN

WHEN Herbert Hoover was sworn into the Presidency in March, 1929, everyone was talking about the stock market. Taxi drivers told about "the tip I got." Bellboys told guests what was happening in the market that day. Bank presidents, elevator boys, housewives were watching the market.

To understand what goes on in the stock market, one must know how American business works. When money is needed for expansion in business or industry, the company gets it from the people by selling shares of stock in the business. When the company makes a profit, it pays a dividend on each share to its stockholders. Thus the American public shares in American business profits. When a company looks as if it will make a lot of money, the prices of its shares go up, and a stockholder may sell his investment for much more than he paid for it. This, too, is the American public sharing the success of American business.

A stock exchange is a market where shares are bought and sold. Someone sells his stock because he is taking a profit or wants to use the money otherwise. Someone buys that same stock because he believes it will go higher. There must be a buyer for every share of stock before it can be sold, and this buying and selling goes on every day in millions of shares in hundreds and thousands of companies. The major stock exchange is in New York.

The prices are made by the people who are buying and selling. When more want to buy, the prices go up. When more people wish to sell, the prices go down. No one can say that the price of any certain stock will go up or down. Hence the stock market reflects the opinion of hundreds of thousands of people. Some of them are informed, honest, and cautious. Some of them are

158

greedy. Some of them are reckless, taking great risks for great profits—or great losses. Some are dishonest. Some are foolish optimists, believing that if some stocks are rising all will rise. Some are pessimists, believing that sooner or later all stocks will go down. The activity of all these people keeps the markets moving, up and down, back and forth.

In the nineteen-twenties, the market was very active, rising in great jumps, dropping in deep slumps. Mostly it was going up so often and so far that men believed it would always go up. In six months in 1929, General Electric stock had gone from $128 a share to $396. Montgomery Ward had soared from $132 to $406. The year before, the selling record had been less than four million shares in one day. In 1929, eight million shares were traded in one day.

Gambling in the market became a feverish game. People in big and little business, schoolteachers, railroad porters, waitresses, people who had never had money in their lives before were playing the game, talking about the game, telling each other what to buy and sell. Many were borrowing money to play the market.

One of the rules of the game was that one could buy stocks by paying only twenty-five percent of the cost in cash. Some brokers let customers buy on a "margin" of ten percent: buy a thousand dollars worth of stock for a hundred dollars down and pay the rest out of profits. People were talking about the beggar who had started with a few thousand dollars and made a quarter of a million. Everyone dreamed of becoming a millionaire. Look at Radio—up from $94 a share to $400!

Hoover had known for four years that there were soft spots in the economy and that this gambling fever was dangerous. He had warned the bankers in 1925 about controlling the speculating and they had called him a killjoy. He had appealed to President Coolidge to speak out against the hysterical gambling in the stock market. Mr. Coolidge had said it was not the President's business to interfere with the country's business. Just before he left office in March, 1929, Mr. Coolidge told the country that "stocks are cheap at current prices," and hearing this from the outgoing President, the people bought, sold, and borrowed faster than ever.

When Hoover was inaugurated, the market went up and up again. In his first message to Congress, President Hoover asked for an examination of the whole banking system of the country and for laws to reform and strengthen it. Most of the money for the stock-market gambling was being borrowed through the banks.

The business of banks is to use the money people put into savings accounts to lend, at interest, to business and industry. As savings thus go out to business, they become wages for workers. The health of the economy depends on this constant circulation of money.

Because the money is working like this, banks can never pay out to all depositors at once all the money in their savings accounts. When depositors become alarmed about the safety of their bank and all crowd to take out their money at the same time, the bank must close its doors. It has failed, and the depositors have lost the money they had in it.

The safety of a bank depends on the management. If the management is dishonest, the money can be stolen. If the management is incompetent, the money can be lost through poor judgment. It is the business of bankers to know what loans are safe and to refuse to make loans that are unsafe.

In 1929 there were no government controls over banks: no inspection of their books, no insurance for deposits, no rules about the kinds of loans they could make. Some of the banks were speculating themselves in the stock market with their depositors' money, and there were no laws to stop them.

Hoover knew these weaknesses and he sent a banking bill to Congress that would correct them. Congress refused to do anything about the banks. Then he tried other ways to stop the speculation. He sent a distinguished bank president on a special mission to New York to warn the bankers and promoters of increasing dangers in the stock-market frenzy. They laughed at the warning, and one of the New York bankers sent back a sharp message to the President: he could undermine the confidence of the whole country talking that way.

President Hoover called in Richard Whitney, Vice President of the New York Stock Exchange, and asked for his cooperation in slowing down the activity in the market. Mr. Whitney promised everything the President asked for. He returned to New York and did nothing.

The federal government had no power to regulate the New York Stock Exchange. The only authority over the stock market in New York was the Governor of New York, Franklin D. Roosevelt. He, too, did nothing.

Of the vast program President Hoover had outlined for the country in his campaign, the farm problem was the most pressing. Six weeks after his inauguration, the President called the Congress into special session to work on it.

Hoover's goal for the farmers was to show them a way in which farmers as businessmen could get a fair profit from their production and maintain the farm way of life with as high a standard of living as any other group of workers. Their problem was very complex: it involved transportation rates, mortgage money, marketing prices, and surplus production.

Two farm organizations, the National Grange and the American Farm Bureau Federation, wanted the government to buy the surpluses at fair market prices and dispose of them. Neither of the farm organizations wished any control of production.

Hoover believed that no government agency should be involved in the buying and selling and price-fixing of any products. This would lead only to greater surpluses and government control. He believed that the farmers could organize to fight their own battles and that government's role was to help them organize.

Congress passed his Agricultural Marketing Act promptly and the Federal Farm Board was established in June, 1929. The Farm Board would help farmers to form marketing organizations, establish elevator associations for storage, and have a fund of one-half billion dollars to "stabilize" market conditions by holding surpluses off the market to wait for more favorable prices. Its purpose was to help the farmer help himself.

Opponents of the bill criticized it for not controlling surplus production. They believed that some kind of federal export (dumping) of surplus farm production was the only answer. Hoover's own answer for surplus production was to take the marginal lands out of production, as he had proposed when he was Secretary of Commerce. Secretary of Agriculture Hyde was collecting information and making plans for the best way to do so by paying the farmer a kind of rent for leaving his land fallow without buying it from him outright.

In the meantime Hoover asked Congress to take up the question of the tariff on agricultural products. The American farmer, he said, was entitled to the American market without competition.

The tariff is the schedule of customs duties or taxes on imports and some exports. The duties were imposed for two reasons: to protect industry and agriculture in the United States from the competition of lower costs abroad where living standards were lower, and to raise revenue for the government.

About two-thirds of the imports in 1929 came in duty-free, such as raw materials for industry. Of the other third, half were agricultural products in competition with the American farmer, and a quarter were luxury goods, taxed only for revenue. No one argued about the need for the tariffs on these two classes of goods.

Thus, of all imports, only about ten percent of the list formed the ground for the argument between "free traders" and "protectionists." This argument had gone around and around, ever since the Administration of George Washington, whose first piece of legislation was a tariff act. Hoover hoped the Congress would leave this ground unbroken. He asked them to consider only the agricultural tariff, and to strengthen the Tariff Commission, with the authority to adjust rates by as much as fifty percent in consultation with the President. This would be a "flexible tariff."

The Congress, however, determined upon a general tariff revision. As the debate went on, many senators inserted new rates into the tariff bill to protect industries in their own states where their votes came from. At the same time they were telling the country at large that the tariff bill was going to raise rates sky high, blaming others for these higher rates. Hoover had hoped this piece of legislation would be out of the way before the regular session opened in the fall. But the Senate became entangled in debating thousands of items, and then they began to oppose the flexible tariff clause. The debate went on into the fall, while the stock market reached new peaks and the gambling fever grew hotter.

On Thursday, October 24, 1929, seven months after Hoover was inaugurated, the stock market crashed. General Electric lost $32.00 a share that day, Montgomery Ward lost $33.00.

By afternoon on that Thursday, some buyers thought the prices were a bargain and began to buy. The market had fallen like this on other days and then had risen higher than ever. Almost thirteen million shares were traded that day. Through Friday and Saturday the market looked better. Prices held fairly steady.

But on Monday the market went down again, though bankers went on telling everyone there was nothing to worry about. Nine million shares were traded, and sometimes there were no buyers, and prices fell ten and fifteen dollars a minute.

Tuesday was even worse. Sixteen million shares were traded in the worst panic in the entire history of the stock exchange. This time the market was not going to come back.

President Hoover knew that this collapse of the stock market was going to affect business. He could not tell how bad it would be but he wanted to assure the people that the country could go on working. He showed a cheerful confidence in the economy as a whole and assured the public that normal business operations could go on.

But in the privacy of his own office he was considering how far the President could go in dealing with depression. He determined that the federal government could take the lead in trying to prevent some of the disasters that could develop in this crisis.

Because no other President had ever dealt with economic depression, there was no experience to look back to, no guidelines to follow. This was a new kind of disaster in which Hoover must pioneer. He said much later, "We could have done better in retrospect."

The President kept giving statements of confidence to the people: pessimism from the President would only make everyone believe things were hopeless. Prosperity and hard times were largely states of mind. If people were confident, courageous, and unfearful, they could keep the economy moving. They still had to eat, to heat their homes, to have clothing, education, and other necessities, and those things had not been touched. Businessmen kept telling each other and the newspapers that the storm had blown over and everything was fine. No banker, no business leader, no expert in any field knew how serious or how long the depression might be.

In the meantime, there was war on another front: a continuing attack that President Hoover could neither ignore, reply to, challenge, nor counterattack.

When the Democrats lost the election in 1928, they began working at once for a victory in 1932. The obvious thing to do was to break down public confidence in Hoover as a great executive, a driving worker, or even an intelligent man.

They proceeded to hire a brilliant newspaperman as publicity director for the Democratic National Committee. An article in Scribner's Magazine in September, 1930, said: "The goal set for him was to 'smear' Mr. Hoover and his administration. That is what he is there for and all he is there for . . ."

He wrote hundreds of interviews, statements, and speeches which members of Congress signed gladly, because of the priceless publicity he gave them. Articles deriding Hoover's abilities, ostensibly by Democratic leaders and members of Congress, appeared in papers and magazines, large and small, across the country.

Darling cartoon during the period of Hoover's vilification

Speeches against Presidential policy were made in Congress. Cooperating newspapers printed editorials, news items, jokes, cartoons ridiculing the President—everything he said, or planned to do, or did do, was labeled as stupid, insane, inept, or ridiculous.

When Hoover tried to curb the speculation in stocks, he was called a dangerous pessimist. When the stock market crashed, men who should have known better ignored Hoover's earlier recognition of, and attempts to rectify, the dangerous financial situation and blamed him alone for the crash. They distorted his failings and blew them up so that he looked not only ridiculous but dangerous. His good qualities went unmentioned.

They tried hard to find scandal in Hoover's early life. Someone accused the President of having stolen $100,000,000 of relief funds during the period of the armistice negotiations. Such an idea was so horrendous that even some of those who had opposed him denied the story and defended him. But the defenses were of little use. The story of Hoover's making good the embezzlement in his London firm was turned into a story that blamed Hoover for the embezzlement. When the Lindbergh baby was kidnapped, it was whispered that Hoover had helped Lindbergh frame the story for publicity. When a Swedish millionaire committed suicide after bankruptcy, it was said that he was a "friend of Hoover." Denials of such stories never achieve the widespread publicity that the stories themselves do, because denials are not sensational.

President Hoover stood virtually alone during those dreadful months. For political reasons, the Democrats attacked him and the Republicans did not protect or defend him. His personal friends marveled at his ability to stand aloof and absorb in silence the punishment he was being given. But the President refused to reply to his attackers, because he believed that in doing so he would lower the dignity of the Presidency.

"I can't take the time from my job to answer such stuff," he said. "If the American people wish to believe such things as this about me, it just cannot be helped."

Nevertheless, he was deeply hurt and disturbed, and he occasionally showed his hurt in angry and exasperated remarks. When he did, his enemies called him thin-skinned.

It was a terrible time not only for the President, but also for the entire country. As the lies spread, the people began to lose confidence in the President, and the country slipped deeper and deeper into a black depression.

SIXTEEN

THE PRESIDENT knew within the first week of the crash that the results would be much more serious than any financial expert had reported. The press urged the President to give out an encouraging statement about the stock market. He refused to discuss the market. All he would say on October 25, after the first bad break, was, "The fundamental business of the country, that is, production and distribution, is on a sound and prosperous basis." No one remarked that he did not include the banking and financial institutions in that statement.

Within three weeks, believing the situation to be extremely critical, the President called conferences of business and labor and industrial leaders to the White House to work out solutions for the unemployment Hoover anticipated. He told the business leaders, on November 21, that he considered the crisis much more than a stock-market crash; there would be a depression and no one could measure the depth of the disaster before them nor its duration. They must all expect a long and difficult period at best.

The immediate problem, he told them, was unemployment. In other depressions the policy had been to "liquidate" labor: let unemployment hit whom it might until the depression reached bottom.

But Hoover had never regarded labor as a commodity to be bought, sold, or discarded. "Labor" meant people: men with families to be fed, homes to be paid for, children to be cared for, men needing jobs. And the jobs must be where the men were living.

As he had done in the depression of 1921, he asked for cooperation from the business and industrial leaders in sharing the work, reducing wages only as the cost of living fell, and letting profits instead of wages take the first shock. The President was aiming at the kind of national cooperation he had received when he had asked the country to save food during the World War. He believed that the voluntary response of individuals to national need was the basis for democratic government.

The leaders of business and industry and the trade associations representing commerce and agriculture, construction and transportation, responded as he had expected. Optimistic plans for spending and building, suggestions for individual homeowners to "buy now while prices are low" were presented to the public by business leaders as well as by government spokesmen. Wages were going to stay up and business was going to go on regardless of the stock market.

For a few months, into the spring of 1930, it seemed as if this program of voluntary cooperation was working: in April a nation-wide census showed only two and a half million unemployed; wages were at their former levels; there had been no strikes.

Unfortunately, some few business concerns did not feel bound by the White House conferences, and scattered reports showed wage cuts and layoffs. Still, on May 1, the President could tell the United States Chamber of Commerce that for the first time in the history of depressions there had been no substantial reductions in wages.

He also said, "We are not through the difficulties of our situation, but I am convinced we have passed the worst, and with continued effort we shall rapidly recover."

His enemies shouted, "The President says prosperity is just around the corner!" This was not what the President had said. But prosperity failed to develop, and the phrase was used for years afterward to ridicule Hoover.

In June the Senate finally sent its tariff bill to the President. Representatives of the farm organizations, the American Federation of Labor, and the National Association of Manufacturers urged him to sign it. Economists and banking men urged him to veto it. The President himself was not satisfied with the Smoot-Hawley bill, named for the legislators who had sponsored it. But the bill had been in debate and the country in uncertainty about it for eighteen months; to continue the uncertainty at this time was most undesirable. The bill did provide the protection for agriculture that Hoover had promised, and it contained the flexible tariff provision he had demanded. Unfair rates could be adjusted without going back to Congress. The President signed the bill.

The months of political agitation and greed, the publicity attacking the bill as a monstrosity, and the spectacle of the United States Senate wrangling for more than ten months over the tariff bill reflected upon the President. People were saying this had been his first test of political leadership and Hoover had failed.

A Washington correspondent had reported, halfway through the Senate debate, "It is now fairly clear that the President will never be a great party leader, because he is not a party man; his mind is essentially nonpartisan, which explains his strength in the country and his weakness in Congress."

But the country was reading all the opposition reports saying that the President was doing nothing, and people were beginning to wonder just what he was doing about the depression.

In August, 1930, the Big Drought struck the Great Plains states. A million farmers watched the skies for rain that never fell and saw their crops die under a blazing sun. Twenty million cattle roamed the ranges looking for water and grew thin without it.

The Democrats cried that Hoover had caused the depression in the first place, and the drought was just another part of the depression. Why did the President not do something?

Hoover was not going to take the time to tell the country what he was doing. He was working out help for the farmers. He asked Congress for money for seed loans for the next year's crops and they passed the bill at once. He got mortgage and insurance companies to extend mortgages so that farmers would not lose their farms. He directed federal departments to concentrate on construction in the drought-stricken states for jobs for farmers. He met with the governors of those states to work out relief plans for farm families.

World prices of wheat dropped that summer and American prices followed. Cotton dropped from eighteen cents a pound in September, 1929, to less than twelve cents a pound by July, 1930, and then continued falling. The Farm Board's efforts to keep American prices up were sharply criticized, and Republican and Democratic senators brought up farm relief bills to raise or guarantee prices. No one could agree on any proposal, and farmers were becoming frustrated and angry with the Republican Administration.

While Hoover worked with the problems of the farmers, prices of other products had been falling and employers were beginning to cut back production. By October, four million men were out of jobs. The President moved as soon as the figures came in to set up a Committee for Unemployment Relief. On October 17 he announced to the press: "As a nation we must prevent hunger and cold to those of our people who are in honest difficulties."

This was a new and enlarged concept of national obligation, a principle in federal government which cut across all the precedents of the past: that the federal government should be responsible for the organization of relief on a nationwide basis. Hoover was the first President to take aggressive leadership in bringing his country through a financial crisis.

His concept of organization for relief called for centralized ideas carried out by groups decentralized in both authority and administration. States, counties, and municipalities set up relief committees that could distribute funds to the needy, and report special problems, beyond local solution, to the federal government. These committees relied on volunteer help because, Hoover said, this would avoid the starry-eyed dreamers, the planners dedicated to experiment, those who would make profit from misery and those who played politics with relief, and also would cut red tape. Furthermore, these volunteers could tell best what was needed in their own community, and they were temporary: when the need was gone, the committee would dissolve.

By November the progressive bloc in Congress was clamoring for the President to abandon his program and offer direct federal aid to the people. This he refused to do. He saw, in direct federal aid to individuals, open opportunities for political corruption; the weakening of the morale of the American people—who thus far were sturdily taking care of their own problems—as well as the weakening of the powers of the states.

These were important aspects of the American way of life to the President, and he was fighting to preserve them in the midst of disaster. His opponents argued that none of these considerations mattered so long as hungry people were fed. Hoover said hungry people could be fed and the unemployed cared for without breaking down the American system of government. When municipalities and states ran out of resources, the federal government would vote money that the states could administer locally.

Progressive opponents brought bills to the Congress to force a "dole" for the people: outright payments of money toward which the people had not contributed through taxes or savings. Hoover fought the bills and, when they failed to pass, the senators cried out to the public that he was heartless about suffering.

By now there was argument over everything Hoover did in fighting the depression. When he pushed the public-works program to make jobs for men, the Democrats and the Old Guard Republicans blamed him for such extravagance in government spending. When he refused to support a bill, politically motivated, to give the Red Cross millions of dollars they said they did not need, then the President was called callous about suffering. He fed the Belgians and Germans and won't feed his own people, his enemies jeered.

This jibe hurt Herbert Hoover more deeply than any other, and this one he answered: "This is not an issue whether people shall go hungry and cold in the United States. It is solely a question of the best method by which hunger and cold shall be prevented."

Whether people should be encouraged to help each other in need or to look the other way while help came from the federal

171

treasury—that was the argument. The people were fighting their own battles successfully, thus far, in the fall of 1930, and the President refused to take the fight away from them.

During that year the Hoovers had their daughter-in-law and grandchildren living with them in the White House, while young Herbert Hoover was hospitalized for ten months with tuberculosis. The President idolized his grandchildren. He took walks with them in the gardens, listened to them chatter, tumbled and wrestled on the floor with them.

He kept candy for them in the top drawer of the Lincoln desk, and tiny Peggy Ann could interrupt his work, order him around, scatter his papers, and he was enchanted with her. He radiated contentment when he walked from the White House to his office with Peggy Ann hanging onto one hand and Peter to the other. They adored their Grandpa, racing to climb into his lap, knowing

Mrs. Hoover with Peggy Ann, Peter, and Mrs. Herbert Hoover, Jr., in 1930

The President and Peggy Ann after attending services at Christ Church, Alexandria, Va.

they could find goodies in the desk drawer, pulling him forcibly from his work to come to lunch.

The country never knew of his enjoyment of his grandchildren. No reporter ever got a human interest story about the children in the White House. The President refused any kind of family publicity for political advantage, and the people never heard of the warm and happy family life behind the President's public life which grew increasingly cold and stern and somber.

His day in the White House began with a game of medicine ball at seven-thirty in the morning. The game was fast and hard, and any number could play. It was played somewhat like volley-ball, with an eight-pound ball tossed over a ten-foot net on a court marked like a tennis court. It was scored like tennis.

This was the President's solution for regular daily exercise, and he invited some official friends and colleagues to join him in the early morning workouts. From six to eighteen would join him every morning, and the group came to be called "the medicine ball Cabinet." Some of the regulars were Harlan Stone, Ray Wilbur, Mark Sullivan, Larry Richey. After the game they had a light breakfast of fruit juice, coffee, and unpolitical conversation.

When his friends had left, the President shaved, bathed, and dressed for the day, and ate a full breakfast while he looked at the papers. At his office he spent the first half hour, from eight-thirty to nine o'clock, on important messages and letters or writing an address. Until nine-thirty he read newspapers carefully and heard staff reports. The rest of the morning he had appointments every fifteen minutes.

At one-thirty the President lunched at the White House, usually with guests, to discuss problems. During the afternoon he had more appointments; and he spent what time he had left in planning, writing, and outlining things to be done next. It was always after six before he left the office.

Dinner at the White House always meant guests: sometimes friends; more often official visitors. The day ended at eleven or twelve at night, and the President was up at six the next morning to begin the new day.

In the spring of 1931, it looked as if the President were winning his battle with depression and unemployment. From February on, employment picked up, payrolls increased, production began to move ahead, bank failures had almost stopped, a hundred and twenty cities reported that relief measures were no longer needed. In spite of the arguments and the name-calling and the bitterness, the country was beginning to move ahead again. Many observers believed and reported that the recession was nearly over.

President Hoover could take a deep breath and think once more of the program he had hoped to carry out for the country. There was time to consider other things than emergency measures. And when he read about the heroic action of a thirteen-year-old school boy in Colorado, the President invited him to visit the White House.

A school bus had run off the road in a blizzard with twenty children trapped inside. The driver had gone off into the blizzard to find aid and had died in the storm.

Bryan Untiedt had saved his classmates, giving them nearly all his own clothes before help came, and he almost lost his own hands and feet from exposure. When he recovered in the hospital, he learned that he had been invited to visit the President.

He arrived on April 29, 1931, with a paper suitcase and a Brownie camera. Mrs. Hoover took him to the garden room where she talked with him, laughing and listening, until he felt at ease. The President received him in his private office, encouraging him to talk at length. At lunch, Bryan was seated next to the President.

He had been invited for one night, but the Hoovers kept him four days, arranging for him to see all the Washington buildings and Mount Vernon. The entire White House staff was captivated with his unselfconscious pleasure and lively interest in everything that was going on. Frequently the President sat down for long conversations with the boy, saying only enough to keep Bryan talking.

Bryan played with the Hoover grandchildren who were visiting at the same time. He took pictures with his camera, he bought souvenirs to take home to his family, and the Hoovers bought him

Mrs. Hoover with Peggy Ann and Peter in 1931

a large leather suitcase in which to carry back all the gifts he had been given.

Ten days after Bryan went home, Europe exploded without warning in a financial earthquake that shook the economic structure of the world. On the New York Stock Exchange prices plunged again.

SEVENTEEN

THE European economies had been unstable for years. Some of the causes lay in the destruction of the World War, and in the Versailles Treaty, which had raised trade barriers between countries. Stock prices on European exchanges had been falling for months before the market in New York collapsed.

In May of 1931, France suddenly demanded from Germany and Austria the money she had loaned to them. Both countries tried to borrow the money to pay France, thus signaling to the world that they were in trouble. Austria's largest bank failed and Europe went into panic. Europeans began selling their American securities on the New York Stock Exchange and prices plunged again.

The American Ambassador to Germany reported that revolution was brewing there: military groups were supporting a man named Hitler. Hardly anyone in America knew who Hitler was: an angry little man with a bristly mustache who shouted that Germany had been stabbed in the back by her own leaders when they had signed the peace treaty of Versailles, that the Jews were to blame for Germany's troubles.

Other countries were in revolution; other governments were falling. Markets for American farm and factory products abroad closed, unemployment was increasing at home and abroad, prices on the Stock Exchange broke again and again. The Soviet Union was dumping wheat, and wheat prices were falling across the world. American wheat prices followed.

Whether the uneasy situation in Europe had primed the depression in America, or the American depression had set off the European collapse, as men argued for years, was unimportant.

The American banking system was so involved with Europe through war debts, bond issues, loans and bank deposits abroad, and European deposits in America, that whatever happened on one side of the ocean affected the other side.

The President moved quickly to strengthen the European banks against collapse. If they failed, American banks would go down with losses that would touch almost every American family.

The weakness of the American banking system was a major cause of the continuing depression. Hoover had recognized this hazard when he was Secretary of Commerce. During those years over five thousand banks failed. In his first message to Congress, after his inauguration, he asked for reforms in the banking laws. Congress ignored his request.

In his second annual message in 1930 he spoke more strongly about the need for strengthening the banking system. Congress paid no attention. That year 1,345 banks had failed.

Now, with European countries collapsing into economic disaster and revolution as well, the American banks were the section of the economy most likely to be overwhelmed. President Hoover refused to explain the danger to newsmen. How could the President, in such a time of crisis and fear, tell his people through the press that their banking system was unstable, irresponsible, and in serious danger of collapse?

But newsmen by now resented Hoover's attitude toward the press. As Secretary of Commerce he had given them stories, told them plans, broken big stories to them, such as the one about the forty-eight-hour week for the steel industry. Newsmen had liked and admired him, and in that friendly atmosphere he was relaxed, warm, and humorous. But the President was very different from the Secretary of Commerce. And the depression was very different from the rosy prosperity of the earlier years. Now he withheld stories that might frighten the people. The press accused him angrily of withholding the news, and this resentment grew into criticism of his leadership, and then his ability, until they began to blame him as much as his political enemies did. So he was a man of facts? Nonsense! Look at the results of all the fact-finding now. He was no statesman, he was thin-skinned and sensitive, he was no politician. A hostile press created a Hoover out of their own dislike, and the public read no defenses of the President. It was difficult even for his friends to make a persuasive explanation of why the country was going from bad to worse.

Hoover knew the picture the public was getting. But protest was futile, and he ignored the publicity while he went on with the work he knew must be done. The European crisis was more important than news stories.

He saw that war debts and reparations were the root of the trouble as, twelve years ago at Versailles, he had feared they would be. Now he proposed that all payments on government debts be suspended between countries for one year to give the European economies a chance to recover.

It was a brilliant stroke, and the editor of a London paper called Hoover by transatlantic telephone within an hour of the announcement to say it was the greatest thing that had happened since the signing of the armistice. The world breathed easier. Confidence revived. The reception of the moratorium on war debts was enthusiastic everywhere except in France.

The French argued for three weeks in favor of using the moratorium to stop paying their own debt to the United States, but not using it to stop collecting their debts from Germany. By the time they agreed to cooperate fully with the moratorium, the early flood of confidence had been shaken. And then in September, 1931, England went off the gold standard.

All prices dropped again in the United States. Other countries began pulling their money out of American banks, reasoning that if England collapsed, America would go next. By October, the American banking system was showing alarming signs of breaking under these pressures from abroad.

Hoover talked with leading bankers about solutions for the

hard-pressed banks, following his principle that with leadership the people could solve their own problems. However, when the bankers showed neither ingenuity, imagination, nor courage, and it became obvious that they were unable to cope with the crisis, Hoover took the first step in putting government into business.

His financial advisers—Eugene Meyer of the Federal Reserve Board, and Ogden Mills, now his Secretary of the Treasury—persuaded him that a federal agency would go far to restore the confidence of the country in the banking system. The President had contemplated such an agency earlier. The time had come to put it into action. He proposed to Congress, in December, 1931, the establishment of the Reconstruction Finance Corporation: the RFC. This organization would make loans to banks, farmers, railways, mortgage agencies, slum-clearance projects, and business; to any financial institutions and operations that could be saved from bankruptcy by government loans. He asked also for the authority to make loans to public institutions and to industries as well as banks, and to credit institutions for agriculture. The opposition in Congress deleted the loan powers for public institutions and for agriculture and delayed the bill in debate for six long weeks. But they passed the bill on January 6 and, in spite of its being less effective than he had hoped, the President signed the bill and the corporation began its work at once.

The RFC performed impressively. Within the next six months it had lent more than eight hundred million dollars to over four thousand institutions which would have failed without that help. This agency was President Hoover's chief contribution to recovery, and in establishing it he put the federal government into business—something he had been entirely opposed to when he had taken office. In making this decision, he was acting swiftly to counter the dangers in the only manner which would work—through the federal government.

In that same session of Congress, Hoover presented a legislative program for the reform of the banking system, the bankruptcy laws, and the New York Stock Exchange. He also called for more money to expand federal public works across the country for further relief.

While they passed his RFC legislation, the Congress rejected the President's banking legislation again. And between the Congress and the President there was a continuing battle over relief. His policies were based on two principles: that it was the responsibility of neighbors, communities, and states to take care of their own needs; and that the credit of the government rested upon a balanced budget, if at all possible; hence it was his obligation to fight the use of funds from the United States Treasury that might be used with any suspicion of political purpose or vote-buying. This kind of legislation was called "pork-barrel."

When bills came to the Congress calling for federal funds

Free lunch lines for hungry people in Chicago

Homeless men lived under city bridges and viaducts

for relief, Hoover was convinced that many of these bills were purely political, and he opposed them. Unquestionably many congressmen and senators could see political gains from giving federal money to their own districts and states. Others, however, had figures about unemployment and hunger that differed from the President's own figures, and they genuinely believed the federal government must take on the obligation of feeding the people.

By the winter of 1931/32, the states were running out of funds. Most of them were prohibited by their constitutions from giving state aid to local communities or from raising taxes to cover relief needs. Social workers and public-welfare officials reported to Senate committee hearings on situations their local communities could not take care of.

Hoover could not believe the states had used up their funds, that they could not issue bonds to raise money, that they could not raise taxes. He could not believe the American people had reached a place where they could not handle their own problems as they had done before.

He was reflecting, in large measure, the temper of his time. The country as a whole believed in a balanced budget and held that the federal government had no business interfering with the affairs of the states or taking care of them. When the President opposed measures for federal relief that would cause huge deficits in the national budget, Congress supported him. But the debate went on. People took sides, the argument was bitter, and the country saw the President as someone who did not care if people went cold and hungry. They had lost their faith in their President, but he would not give up easily his faith in the strength, ingenuity, and endurance of the American people.

Nor would he compromise by a jot his determination not to be any kind of hero, not to let the press show the people anything warm and personal about him, not to explain what he was doing. He tried not to care what people thought, but he could not help caring, and he grew irritable and brusque with newsmen who badgered him with questions about delicate problems.

In December, 1931, at the same time the Congress was deleting the President's request for extra powers in the RFC legislation, Senator Edward P. Costigan of Colorado and Robert M. La Follette of Wisconsin introduced a bill providing for federal aid to the needy. Social workers, labor leaders, clergymen, and others who were close to the needy testified about the growing helplessness of the private organizations and communities to cope with the need.

The senate debated the bill at length and defeated it. Hoover had opposed the bill, hence the defeat was a victory for the President. He was not convinced that the states had exhausted their resources. This was something hard to prove either way. His decision to fight the Costigan-La Follette bill, in the late period of the depression, was probably his greatest mistake during his fight for recovery.

In July, a relief bill was at last presented which Hoover could approve: the Emergency Relief and Construction Act. This act permitted financially exhausted states to borrow from the RFC for public works. The advantages of this bill, in Hoover's opinion,

President Hoover and his cabinet in 1932: (Seated, left to right) Ogden L. Mills, Secretary of the Treasury; Charles Curtis, Vice President; the President; Henry L. Stimson, Secretary of State; Patrick J. Hurley, Secretary of War; (Standing) Roy D. Chapin, Secretary of Commerce; Ray Lyman Wilbur, Secretary of the Interior; William D. Mitchell, Attorney General; Walter F. Brown, Postmaster General; Charles F. Adams, Secretary of the Navy; Arthur M. Hyde, Secretary of Agriculture (these last five were members of the President's original cabinet); William N. Doak, Secretary of Labor

were that it would be administered by local communities or states, it would not take the providing of relief away from private agencies, and the states would repay the borrowed money in better times instead of getting a gift from the government.

That July the depression reached its lowest point. There were 12,400,000 people unemployed, 18,000,000 on relief. Congress suddenly felt they had delayed long enough and passed several of the President's bills, including the Home Loan Bank Bill, which would help homeowners to get money to carry their mortgages and keep their homes. Congress then adjourned without any action on the banking reform.

But President Hoover had accomplished a greater part of his total program than he had dared to hope for. He had demonstrated, in both the bills he pushed through and the bills he had opposed and vetoed, a political strength and effectiveness that has long been underestimated.

His major handicap was that he was the first President to break a new path in an unknown situation, to face and try to solve staggering new problems. He had no examples to look back to, no records to consult. He had to figure out for himself the direction to take.

With the adjournment of Congress, the whole country felt as if a cloud of uncertainty had lifted. Stocks began to gain, farm prices rose, payrolls went up, unemployment went down, production moved ahead. At the same time the depression in Europe had reached its low point, and business there started up again. Recovery was on the way in the world at last.

EIGHTEEN

NINETEEN THIRTY-TWO was a Presidential election year. The Republican Convention was meeting in Chicago in June, and the Republicans had a problem—they had the Republican President.

They had not wanted Hoover for their candidate in 1928, and now they were embarrassed in 1932. They had done nothing to defend their President against Democratic smears, and now they had begun to believe the smears themselves. How could they work for a man who, according to the Democrats, had caused the depression and then had done nothing for four years?

And yet it would be even more embarrassing for the party to tell the country that their choice for President had been a mistake. So with very little intention of electing him, the Republican Party nominated Herbert Hoover again.

Two weeks later, the Democratic Convention, also in Chicago, nominated Franklin D. Roosevelt. The Democrats had been divided about their candidate too, but when he was nominated they closed ranks behind him, determined to win the election they had been fighting for since 1929.

During the summer, the world had turned from depression to recovery, and the President went into the campaign to tell the people what he had done during his Administration. In spite of a hostile Congress, the continuing attack on his name and reputation, and three years of deepening depression, President Hoover had a remarkable record of permanent accomplishment for the American people.

The candidates, in their campaign speeches, wrangled over depression and relief, and the Democratic candidate said in a dozen different ways that the Republican President had done

186

nothing. It was true that Hoover had failed in some of his important programs. The Senate had refused to act on the Marginal Lands Act and the farm problem was as bad as ever. He had not been able to get his banking reform legislation. Congress had blocked the bill to reorganize the executive branch of government.

But he was the first President in America's history to mobilize the economic resources of the people to fight a depression. A million workers had gone back to their jobs since June, 1932, and others were returning at the rate of half a million a month by September. Farmers were better off in 1932 by a billion dollars. Thousands of men had been working through the depression on the Hoover Dam, now three-quarters completed, the biggest dam in the world.

During his Administration President Hoover had completed plans for the Grand Coulee Dam, second only to the Hoover Dam; for four other dams on the great rivers in the Central Valley of California; for flood control along a thousand miles of the Mississippi River; and he had persuaded the Congress to pass the legislation for rivers and harbor works in a national plan which would move forward for the next ten years. He had signed the treaty with Canada for the St. Lawrence Waterway on July 13, and it needed only the approval of the Senate for the work to begin.

Under his Administration, the acreage of national forests and parks had increased by over five million acres. The airmail service had been reorganized, early in 1930, to carry passengers as well as mail. By 1933, passenger service and mileage had tripled, and net costs per mile had been cut by eighty percent. He had opened airmail to South America, which later led to the establishment of Pan American Airways.

He had worked out the engineering of the San Francisco Bay Bridge and used RFC funds for its building, as a constructive public work to give employment. The tolls repaid the RFC funds when the bridge was finished, and the greatest bridge in the world, at that time, was built without cost to the government.

He had set in motion a national program for building homes

and clearing slums, and he had worked for legislation to protect the children of America. Child mortality dropped each year during the depression from 6,880 deaths per hundred thousand in 1928 to 5,760 per hundred thousand in 1932. Hoover personally had written a Children's Charter, calling for the protection of the rights of every child under the American flag, regardless of race, color, or situation.

He had made reforms in the proceedings of justice and in bankruptcy practice to help small businessmen and homeowners. He had reorganized the FBI under J. Edgar Hoover. He had sent to Congress legislation for the most enlightened and extensive reform in dealing with criminals in the history of the federal government, and it had been passed by Congress.

In foreign affairs, the President had led the United States to greater cooperation with world moral forces for peace, with the Hoover-Stimson Doctrine which stated that the United States would not recognize territories gained by force. He had set up a World Economic Conference for the spring of 1933 to stabilize currencies and help world trade. He had developed a Good Neighbor policy with Latin America and withdrawn American troops from Nicaragua and Haiti. Latin American relations were more cordial at the close of his administration than at any time since 1901.

The fact that he could keep all these goals in sight and accomplish so much during the crises and continuing emergencies was the real measure of his vision, his political strength, and his leadership.

But all these achievements, valuable and important as they were for the country, were not the stuff of drama for campaigns. They were the results of hard, concentrated, steady, slogging work—and who wanted to hear about work in a campaign where crowds were shouting, bands were playing, flags were flying, and Franklin Roosevelt was crying, "We cannot go back to children working in factories"?

The crowds forgot that Hoover had urged the adoption of the

Child Labor Amendment to the Constitution since 1920 and that the state where Roosevelt was governor had refused to act upon it at all.

Roosevelt said, "Over six million of our schoolchildren are fainting in the classroom from hunger!" City administrations protested the lie. Health services reported the facts. But who hears the truth when the lie is so fascinating?

Roosevelt cried, "I want to say with all the emphasis that I can command that this Administration did nothing, and their leaders, I am told, are still doing nothing about the depression!" He said, "The Administration lined up with the stock market. . . . It encouraged speculation . . . it refused to recognize and correct the evils . . . it delayed relief; it forgot reform. . . ."

The people who had read the same charges in the papers for three years were convinced that the man who had been the Great Humanitarian and the Great Administrator four years ago was now cold-hearted, callous to suffering, unable to act, and doing nothing.

Hoover told the people exactly what he had done. He wrote his own speeches; no ghost spoke for him. His attack on Roosevelt's weakness and lack of purpose was hard-hitting and accurate, his defense of his own Administration was superb. But his campaign was keyed to reason instead of drama and to fact instead of colorful emotion.

Roosevelt was a new man with a charming personality, an infectious smile, a golden voice. And who listens to reason when emotion is so much more exciting?

The American people, tired of the depression, fretful with the slow progress of recovery, angry with the bickering of the Republicans and a "do-nothing Administration," and charmed with the gaiety and confidence of the Democratic candidate, elected Franklin D. Roosevelt in November, 1932.

Herbert Hoover was through with the campaign but he was not through with the Presidency. The country must keep on running from November until March, and the one who must keep his hand on the wheel was the defeated President.

On his way back to Washington from California where he had voted, President Hoover stopped to see the work at the great dam at Boulder, Colorado. It was higher than the Washington Monument. He himself had worked out the agreement between the states. He had drafted the legislation for the sale of the electrical power so the entire cost of the dam should be returned to the government. The work had finally begun while he was President and it was now three-fourths finished.

The Secretary of the Interior had named it the Hoover Dam, when work began in 1930, following the custom of naming dams for the Presidents in whose terms they were built. No other President—Theodore Roosevelt, Woodrow Wilson, or Calvin Coolidge—had taken more than a casual interest in the dams named for them.

But the Hoover Dam meant to President Hoover an engineering project that was as much his own as anything he had done in his professional career, the most tangible result of his service to his country, and the achievement that would continue benefiting mil-

Filling the Hoover Dam at Boulder, Colorado

lions of people for decades after he left the White House. When he left the Hoover Dam towering under the stars, he was going back to the last four months in office, which were to be the hardest part of his whole term.

The four-month lapse between election and inauguration at that time was called the "interregnum"—the time between rulers. The outgoing President had no power because he had been defeated. The incoming President had no real power until his inauguration. But he had the political and psychological power of his victory, and he could use that power to cooperate with the outgoing President or to block any further accomplishment.

The recovery of the summer had begun to fade in September when Maine voted for Roosevelt. It was slipping into depression by November, and when Hoover was defeated the depression quickened into panic.

Roosevelt said the country was afraid of the old system; Hoover pointed out that the country could not be afraid of a man going out of office in four months.

He hoped to use those four months to stabilize the economy and check the fears of the people. Most problems could still be solved before March fourth if the new President would work with him. He invited Roosevelt to a conference on war debts and foreign affairs.

It was a difficult meeting for both men. Roosevelt was uneasy and nervous. Hoover was cold and glum. Roosevelt was wary of being drawn into anything that might commit him to Hoover's policies, and he was convinced that Hoover's advisers were trying to trap him into a commitment to the old ways. Hoover did not feel that Roosevelt understood any of the problems or cared about the explanations.

Roosevelt believed the most important thing was the depression at home and domestic policies that would solve it. Hoover believed the Economic Conference and an adjustment of the war debts which would help Europe get on its feet would help the American economy at home. Each man resented the other's attitude. There was no basis of understanding between them at all. Roosevelt refused to agree, to disagree, or to propose any solutions of his own for anything.

Hoover went back to work with the Congress as if he were entering the Presidency instead of leaving it, and his enemies criticized him for that. He urged the Senate to ratify the treaty for the St. Lawrence Waterway, so the work could begin and more jobs would be open. He asked the Congress to help the farmers. He urged them, for the sixth time, to pass the banking reform legislation. But Congress was not interested in the program of an outgoing President.

The Senate debated the question of relief all over again. Witnesses testified that more people were cold and hungry and sick than the Department of Public Health realized. The Senate criticized every principle of relief that Hoover believed in. But still it did nothing for the sick and hungry people.

And then there was the problem of money which made people across the country very uneasy indeed.

Money has many different properties. It is "tight" when you must pay high interest rates to borrow it. It is "easy" when interest rates are low. It is "hard" when it is silver. It is "soft" when it is paper. It is "sound" when there is a certain proportion of gold held in the United States vaults behind the paper money in circulation. The proportion that law requires today is one dollar in gold for four dollars in paper. When foreign countries wish to exchange dollars for gold, the gold must be paid out. This is "the gold standard."

Economists who try to explain why business and money and credit and gold act as they do have different opinions among themselves about the reasons. Politicians form their opinions from the economists they talk to.

In the interregnum, Roosevelt talked about inflating the currency. This means making dollars cheaper by changing the value of the gold behind the dollars. It is also called "tinkering with the currency."

When dollars are cheaper, more of them are needed to buy anything. Inflation means that prices go up, wages rise, and everyone has more dollars to spend. Hoover and his advisers believed that, once started, inflation would be very hard to stop. Germany had printed paper money without gold behind it in 1923, and it took a million marks to buy a postage stamp before the inflation had ended.

Rumors began spreading that Roosevelt might change the gold standard, and there was no telling what he was going to do to the money of the country. People began to hoard gold and silver in safe-deposit boxes instead of savings accounts. Rich people sent their gold out of the country to banks in Europe where they thought it would be safer than in America. By the middle of February people were taking $15,000,000 a day out of the banks. By the end of February a thousand banks had closed holding $200,-000,000 in deposits. Sound banks were closing because people were afraid now of all banks. The country was on its way to a real panic.

President Hoover prepared to proclaim a law that would restrict people from withdrawing their money, which would have stopped the panic. But such a proclamation required the consent of Congress, and Congress would not pass it without the agreement of the President-elect. Roosevelt did not agree.

In deep disgust, President Hoover declared that this banking panic was the most senseless and most easily prevented panic in history. There was nothing more the outgoing President could do.

On March 4, 1933, he went to his office for the last time. It was a raw and cloudy morning, and at eleven o'clock the new President would be inaugurated.

Hoover knew he had been the most criticized President since Lincoln. Perhaps he drew some comfort in knowing that Lincoln, too, had been derided and rejected by his people. For almost four years the White House had been for him a place where the nights were haunted by things that went wrong, and where any dawn might bring bad news. But as the final hours of the long strain came to an end and release was in sight, Hoover put the problems and stresses out of his mind. They were no longer his. When there was no further stone to turn, he let go of all the worries.

Someone asked him, "Any last words, Mr. President?"

He smiled when he said the air was already full of his words and in a month they'd all be forgotten. The smiles had been rare while he was in office.

He rode in the open car with the incoming President to the Capitol. Crowds cheered and applauded, but Mr. Hoover, with his eyes cast down, paid little attention, believing the applause was not for him.

In the rotunda of the Senate Chamber, the Chief Justice administered the oath of office to the new President, and Franklin D. Roosevelt was inaugurated.

Part VII

The Former President

"I notice in the press a generous suggestion that my countrymen owe to me some debt. . . . On the contrary the obligation is mine. My country gave me, as it gives every boy and girl, a chance. It gave me schooling, the precious freedom of equal opportunity for advancement in life, for service and honor. In no other land could a boy from a country village without inheritance or influential friends look forward with unbounded hope. . . . It gave me the highest honor that comes to man—the Presidency of the United States."

Herbert Hoover, in Hoover After Dinner

Herbert Hoover in 1933 (sketch by Clarence Mattie)

NINETEEN

THE Hoovers went back to live in the house they had built on a hilltop at Stanford. Their lives could be their own again. After nineteen years of public service, private life was freedom from a kind of peonage, and they enjoyed that freedom completely.

They ate breakfast when they wanted to. They read the papers knowing that what was printed there was no longer their responsibility or their fault. They could choose their visitors for pleasure alone. They could walk out the front door and drive into the mountains without leaving some public emergency behind them.

And the former President could go fishing. All his life, fishing was his time of contemplation, of peace, of tranquillity.

He had promised himself that he would give President Roosevelt two years in office without criticism, and for those years he watched public life go by without comment. He was examining his own convictions, and he wrote them out in *Challenge to Liberty.*

Within sixty days of his leaving office, Hoover's name was taken off the Colorado River Dam. The Secretary of the Interior changed the name Hoover Dam to Boulder Dam. When the dam was dedicated in September the President did not invite him to attend.

The Democratic Administration was deeply afraid that Hoover would some day campaign against them again. To forestall this danger, they continued for fourteen years to blacken his name, revile his memory, distort his record, and blame his administration, so that to the American public Herbert Hoover would mean nothing but "Hoover Depression." They were remarkably successful.

Former President Hoover and his dog, Pat, on the terrace of the Stanford home, in 1935

Hoover himself ignored the charges and the rumors. He was used to them now, and they could hurt him no longer. Once, during his Presidency, Hugh Gibson had asked Mrs. Hoover, "How can he take it so calmly?"

She said, as if everyone knew why, "Bert can take it better than most people because he has deeply engrained in him the Quaker feeling that nothing matters if you are 'right with God.' "

Observing his resolution to be a very private citizen for two years, Hoover saw President Roosevelt take the United States off the gold standard and cheapen the dollar; saw him turn the nation

of the city streets. What they needed was a focus for their loyalties and an experience in the virtues of sportsmanship. To this purpose Hoover gave over twenty-five years of service to the Boys' Clubs, and took pride in the fact that when thirty percent of the nation's young men were physically or mentally unfit for draft calls, among the alumni of the Boys' Clubs only four and one-half percent failed to qualify.

In 1938, when war clouds were darkening the world again, Hoover returned to Europe for the first time in twenty years. He wanted to see what had happened to Europe in those years and to find the roots of the conflict that was rushing upon the world.

He was still the best-known and best-loved American in Europe, and everywhere he went he was greeted by crowds and loaded with medals and honors. Streets were named for him. A new asteroid discovered by the Brussels Observatory was named "Herberta" in his honor. Many years before another asteroid had been named "Hooveria" by an Austrian astronomer.

He met leaders with whom he had worked in the past, and he met the new leaders. He found that Europe had generally recovered from the depression. The democracies were prosperous. The only country still lagging was France, which had adopted a New Deal, similar to the New Deal in America. Five years after Hoover had left office, there were twenty-three million Americans on relief.

Eighteen months later, Hitler invaded Poland, and again the Poles were starving. Their government asked the American Friend to get food for them. The Wilson Administration had supported his efforts to feed Belgium in World War I. The Roosevelt Administration opposed any effort to feed Poland in World War II.

Hoover established the Polish Relief Commission as a private citizen, and for two years the commission fed three hundred thousand children in the German-occupied territory until the war stopped private effort.

For the duration of the Second World War, Hoover and his relief committee worked and fought for the children of Europe against the determined opposition of his own government. Con-

toward socialism; saw him strike down the Economic Conference that would have meant so much to world peace.

Following the collapse of the Economic Conference, the dictators in Europe began to arm for war without interference. Hitler became Fuehrer in Germany; Mussolini became Premier in Italy. Their armies began to grow. And in America the depression continued unchecked. Twenty million persons had been on relief when Roosevelt was inaugurated. Two years later, twenty-two million persons were on relief.

Hoover watched these disasters without public comment until March, 1935. Then he began speaking to America again. He spoke, as he had earlier, about individual liberty and responsible government within the Constitution. From that time on he spoke and wrote articles discussing the American Way and the direction it was taking.

In 1936, Hoover became chairman of the board of the Boys' Clubs of America. He had always had a special concern for the children of the world, and he took a special interest in the boys

Mr. Hoover with members of the Boys' Club of America

gress endorsed his plan for feeding the small democracies: Belgium, Holland, Norway, Finland, and Poland. But the State Department refused to cooperate.

Hoover was more bitter about this inhumanity than about any other opposition that he had ever encountered. What were democracy and freedom worth in America if children starved only because the American Administration chose they should not be fed?

He had always opposed American entry into European conflict. He said, "We can make war, but we do not and cannot make peace in Europe."

As the war grew deeper and blacker, Americans began to argue about helping European friends. In the 1940 Presidential campaign Hoover said emphatically that America should stay out of the war. If America stayed neutral she would hold the key to a democratic peace. If America stayed out of war, the dictators of Italy, Germany, and Russia would destroy each other.

He was not alone in these views. But emotions were rising, Hitler had become our enemy, and Hoover was still unpopular with most of the country. When he called for feeding countries now held by Hitler, the people thought he was a sentimental traitor. His standing in the country fell to the lowest point it had ever reached in 1941.

In December, Japan attacked the American fleet at Pearl Harbor. Hoover at once declared that Japan's attack on American soil now forced us to fight with everything we had. He called for full support of the President of the United States in the war, and he offered his complete cooperation with the war effort.

The Democratic Administration ignored him. At no time in the great struggle of the Second World War did they use his help, his advice, his experience, or his great ability. The food situation at home deteriorated. Farm production choked on red tape. Black markets and corruption flourished. But the help of the man who knew more about such problems than anyone else in the world was rejected.

201

Hoover continued working through the war years as a private citizen with his own relief committee and the Red Cross and Friends' Service Committee. He wrote articles about the problems of food conservation and distribution and aroused public opinion enough to make some improvements.

With an old friend of his, former Ambassador Hugh Gibson, who was also shut out of war work, Hoover wrote a book called *The Problems of Lasting Peace*. Published in 1942, the book was widely acclaimed. One journalist called it "nothing less than a state paper." But this contribution, too, was ignored by the twenty government agencies working on the problems of the peace.

In 1941, the Hoover Tower was dedicated on the Stanford Campus, housing the Institution on War, Revolution and Peace, which Hoover had founded in 1919. Hoover himself had contributed $150,000 to the Institution, and friends and institutions collected funds for continuing its work.

The Tower has fourteen levels, holding the largest collection in the world of documents on the Communist, Fascist, Nazi, and Socialist revolutions. Millions of items in eighty-nine different languages provide scholars with an invaluable source of information on the greatest evils the world must cope with: war and revolution. The Institution's holdings on the Russian and Chinese revolutions and the spread of communism through the world are considered to be the outstanding collections in this field in the free world.

In scope and ambition and contribution to the knowledge of his fellow men, the Hoover Institution on War, Revolution and Peace may be the greatest of all his contributions to mankind.

Three years later, in 1944, Hoover suffered the deepest personal blow of all. Lou Henry Hoover died suddenly of heart failure on January 7, a month before their forty-fifth anniversary. When he was going through her papers, Hoover found a last letter addressed to her sons: "You have been lucky boys to have had such a father, and I am a lucky woman to have had my life's trail alongside the path of three such men and boys."

The Hoover Tower, housing the Institution on War, Revolution and Peace at Stanford University

TWENTY

AS the worst war in the world's history approached its end in 1945, Franklin Roosevelt died and Harry Truman became President. Two months after he entered the White House, President Truman invited former President Hoover to the White House. It was the first time Mr. Hoover had entered its doors since he had left office.

In 1946, as postwar famine threatened Europe again, the President asked Herbert Hoover to head the Famine Emergency Commission to study the world crisis and prepare a program to deal with it.

Four veterans from his World War I commission went with him: Hugh Gibson, Perrin Galpin, Maurice Pate, and Hallam Tuck. Dennis FitzGerald of the Department of Agriculture and a topflight journalist, Frank E. Mason, also went with the commission. They surveyed the food needs and resources of twenty-five countries in fifty-seven days of hard travel and fifty-seven nights of hours of work, traveling more than 50,000 miles in an army-transport plane.

During the trip Hoover broadcast his findings in Europe to the people at home. Between twenty and thirty million children were already physically subnormal. It was the cruelly malnourished children of World War I who had followed Hitler into World War II.

Hoover organized the food of the world to sustain several hundred million people until the next harvest, writing out his reports as he went along. At seventy-two his vitality under this crushing pace was formidable. When he reached home his report was ready for the President: a blueprint for feeding the world.

President Truman asks Hoover to head the Famine Emergency Commission (above); Hoover's reception in Greece on the Food Mission (below)

(Above) Hoover meets the homeless children of Warsaw again, in 1946; (Below) A devastated street in Poland

This kind of assignment, a big and vital task involving public need, was always the most helpful tonic for Herbert Hoover's troubles. Alone now, he covered his continuing grief for his wife with activity as great as any in the early years.

A month after his return from the Famine Emergency study, President Truman asked him to make the same survey in Latin America. His explanation of the situation, when he returned, persuaded Congress to vote the huge appropriations the President asked for, to feed the hungry and defeated peoples of the world.

At the end of the year President Truman turned to Hoover again, this time for a survey of the problems of American occupation in Europe. His report on those problems was the basis for the Truman–Marshall plan for Europe. His continuing work in feeding the children evolved into the United Nations International Children's Emergency Fund: UNICEF, which has been one of the more effective departments of the United Nations.

In the spring of 1947, Congress asked Hoover to do the job that President Hoover had tried again and again to do in his own term of office: a study for the reorganization of the executive branch of the federal government. Congress then had refused to pass Hoover's legislation. Now Congress called Mr. Hoover back to direct that very work: to improve economy and efficiency in the White House, to get rid of overlapping services and bureaus, and to define the executive functions, services, and activities.

The job was much bigger now than it would have been twenty years before. Two million people were working in 1,812 different agencies. Seventy-five different bureaus, divisions, and agencies duplicated and crossed up each other's work in transportation alone. More than forty-four agencies were spending money on health and medical services. The government was spending a billion dollars a year just to maintain its records.

The Hoover Commission spent fifteen months in research and then presented for the first time the clear picture of the federal government of the United States and offered 280 individual recommendations in detail.

By the end of the Truman term and in the first Eisenhower year, seventy percent of the recommendations had been adopted by Congress. Mr. Truman considered it one of the most important achievements of his Administration.

While the work of the Hoover Commission was going on, Congressman Jack Z. Anderson introduced a bill to restore Hoover's name to the Colorado dam. Both houses passed the bill almost unanimously.

For the first time that he had taken any recognition of this matter, Hoover expressed his feelings about it in a letter to the congressman and, between the lines, revealed something of his feeling about the character assassination he had endured for fourteen years:

My dear Mr. Congressman:

Thank you for yours of March seventh.

Confidentially, having had streets, parks, schoolhouses, hills and valleys named for me, as is done to all Presidents, I have not thought this item of great importance in the life of a nation. But when a President of the United States tears one's name down, that is a public defamation and an insult. Therefore, I am grateful to you for removing it.

Yours faithfully,

HERBERT HOOVER

The dark years had ended. Americans in 1946 began recalling the things Hoover had stood for through storms of slander, abuse, and hatred. In 1947, a ranking liberal writer, Dr. Alvin Johnson, wrote an open letter to him: "The place of Hoover in history, a most honored place, is that of the man who extended American neighborliness to the world. . . . I do recognize that among the Americans of my time you have been the greatest, by virtue of your extending the concern of Americans to the whole world."

During that summer Hoover attended the annual newspaper publishers' convention in New York. At his entrance the publishers broke into spontaneous ovation, standing and cheering again and again. Hoover was so surprised and touched that he was unable to respond, struggling to hold back tears.

Members of Congress in both parties began to consult Hoover for his views. A Washington paper reported that the former President packed more weight on legislation than any Republican leader outside Congress. Another paper said he was emerging as one of the top economic advisers of the Congress.

As his seventy-fifth birthday approached in 1949, public acclaim reached a high point. Editors in papers across the country spoke of him as "one of the greatest men in American history," "our most distinguished private citizen," "one of the really great American statesmen."

They praised his "contribution to the public welfare, his personal virtues of integrity and constancy in the face of unjust and undeserved belittlement and criticism." They commended "his life of superb usefulness" and "his public service, staunchly built on unshakable moral principle." They said he was "perhaps not fitted for partisan politics, but nevertheless one of our greatest citizens, and one whom history undoubtedly will recognize as one of our greatest Presidents."

It was an astonishing outpouring of recognition and gratitude, often from people who regretted they had not recognized his qualities earlier. Never before had a living former President received such an ovation in the press.

Four years later, President Eisenhower asked him to direct the work for a second Hoover Commission report. This commission was asked to consider policies and functions of the government, as well as its practices. This involved the philosophy of government, and their work was more controversial than the first report. In spite of opposition, the reports have provided guidance for government policies and practice ever since. This report was as solid and complete and bold in its recommendations as the first one. It dealt with fundamental questions of the philosophy of government—what the government should and should not do. The

Hoover family gathering in West Branch, Iowa, on his eightieth birthday. Left to right: Herbert Hoover, III; Herbert, Jr.; Stephen (great grandson); Mr. Hoover; Andrew and Allan, Jr.; Mrs. Allan Hoover; Mrs. Herbert Hoover, Jr.; Mrs. Herbert Hoover, III. Allan Hoover is behind the former President

President Eisenhower holding citation to Mr. Hoover for his contributions to better government, 1957

final report was more controversial than the report of the First Hoover Commission. It recommended that the government step out of many activities that were in competition with private enterprise, and provoked furious criticism from those who favored Big Government.

Hoover was philosophical. He was used to criticism, and he said, "I manage to console myself with the thought: 'Old reformers never die; they get thrown out.'"

He was eighty-one when the report was published, and it was his last important assignment for the government.

But Hoover was not one to "retire." He had work of his own to do, and he plunged into it with undiminished vigor. He intended to keep on working as long as he kept on breathing.

He began writing the record of the tragedy of peacemaking in 1918, history in which he had been present. He wrote with the insight of not only personal experience, but the long perspective of forty years.

The Ordeal of Woodrow Wilson, published in 1958, was widely acclaimed as a major contribution to the history of our time. Historians called it a really large contribution to our knowledge of World War I, and a work of rare importance. The New Yorker called it one of the most remarkable documents of our time. And the magazine of American history, American Heritage, said, "Of all the new books about him, none can match in basic importance The Ordeal of Woodrow Wilson by Herbert Hoover."

Hoover has been recognized for his achievements in his chosen profession of engineering, for his massive accomplishments in saving hundreds of millions of people from famine, for his permanent and valuable gains for the people of America as Secretary of Commerce, and as President of the United States. These contributions were part of his full-time work in each of these fields.

Too little recognition has been given his achievements as historian. Recording history was an avocation running like a golden thread through the warp of both public and private life. Not only did he publish many volumes of history, beginning with the solution to the baffling puzzle of *De Re Metallica*, but he established the immensely important Institution on War, Revolution and Peace, which collects and grows with history itself.

He was eighty-four when *The Ordeal of Woodrow Wilson* was published, and he went on to write the record of American relief, a four-volume history which carried the story from World War I through the famine following World War II, and up to 1963.

An American Epic was published in June, 1964, four months before his ninetieth birthday. At the same time he was working with the Boys' Clubs; working with the Institution on War, Revolution and Peace; accepting invitations to speak; writing magazine articles. A staff of six to eight secretaries and researchers could hardly keep up with him. One secretary said, "The Chief's idea of a vacation is to work eight hours a day instead of sixteen."

He still wrote the first drafts of all his articles and speeches himself in longhand, revising and correcting them before letting a secretary type the final copies. The college freshman who had been conditioned in English and had found composition his most difficult subject had long since learned to write easily and well, with beautiful organization of detail, and droll and unexpected humor.

On his eighty-eighth birthday, on August 10, 1962, the Hoover Presidential Library was dedicated in West Branch, Iowa, and one of his friends organized a party to fly with Hoover in a chartered plane for the occasion. Thousands came to see the famous Elder Statesman and greet him with thundering applause. He looked a little feeble, but his mind was as sharp as ever.

In his address to the gathering there, he spoke of the historical purpose of the Presidential libraries: the Hoover Library was the fourth, following the libraries of President Roosevelt, President Truman, and President Eisenhower. He said, "Within them are thrilling records of supreme action by the American people, their devotion and sacrifice to their ideals.

"Santayana rightly said, 'Those who do not remember the past are condemned to relive it.' These institutions are the repositories of such experience—hot off the griddle."

212

Herbert Hoover, after 1960

His last words in the address were to the boys and girls of America: ". . . the doors of opportunity are still open to you. Today the durability of freedom is more secure in America than in any place in the world."

The next morning a *New York Times* editorial said, "If freedom is today more secure in America than any other place in the world, Herbert Hoover helped to make it so."

When he died, two years later, on October 20, 1964, the American Friend had freely given fifty years of his life to freedom for all men everywhere.

He chose to go back to his early days, to lie near his birthplace on a sunny hill in West Branch. The marble stones for Herbert Hoover and Lou Henry Hoover lie flat and plain under the Iowa sky, the only design of his gravesite drawn in the swelling of the hilltop, the half circle of cedars, and the sweep of the road. In his death as in his life he held to the simplicity of the Friends.

HERBERT HOOVER'S LEGACY
TO HIS COUNTRY

Part of the legacy Herbert Hoover left his country is the record of his philosophy and principles, his own special humor, and his feeling for America.

On Liberalism and Freedom:

"Liberty is a thing of the spirit—to be free to worship, to think, to hold opinions, and to speak without fear. . . . There are stern obligations upon those who would hold these liberties: self-restraint, insistence upon truth, order and justice, vigilance of opinion, and co-operation in the common welfare."

—*Challenge to Liberty*

"The structure of human betterment cannot be built upon foundations of materialism or business, but upon the bedrock of individual character in free men and women."

—*Challenge to Liberty*

"True Liberalism is found not in striving to spread bureaucracy but in striving to set bounds to it."

American Road, 1950/55

On America:

"In my long life I have lived and worked in countries of free men, of tyrannies, of Socialists and Communists. I have seen liberty die and tyranny rise. I have seen slavery again on the march.

"Every one of my homecomings was for me a reaffirmation of

215

the glory of America. Each time my soul was washed by relief from the grinding poverty of many nations, by the greater kindliness and frankness which come from acceptance of equality and wide-open opportunity to all who want a chance. I was inspired by the self-respect born alone of free men. There is no place on the whole earth, except here in America, where every boy and girl can have such a chance."

—*On Growing Up*

"The conviction that every person in the Republic owes a service to the Republic; that the Republic rests solely upon the willingness of every one in it to bear his part of the duties and obligations of citizenship is as important as the ability to read and write—that is the only patriotism of peace."

—*The Hoover Administration*

On the Presidency:

"Why Presidents seldom worry about anything: they have so many troubles in the closet or stowed away in the ice box that when one of them gets tiresome they can always send for another, and by great variety maintain interest and a high cheerfulness of spirit."

—*Hoover After Dinner*, Dec. 12, 1929 following the crash

"(News Censorship) is a thorny subject . . . involving the theory that the principal job of Presidents is to make news for both morning and afternoon editions each day, and particularly that it shall have a mixed flavor of human-interest story and a dog-fight that will please the village gossips."

—*Hoover After Dinner*, Dec. 12, 1931

"Being a politician is a poor profession. Being a public servant is a noble one."

—*On Growing Up*

His Advice to Children, in answering the letters children **wrote:**

To a ten-year-old boy who asked how to get to be President:
"The first rule is just to be a boy, getting all the constructive joy out of life;

"The second rule is that no one should win the Presidency without honesty and sportsmanship and consideration for others in his character—together with religious faith;

"The third rule is that he should be a man of education.

"If you follow these rules you will be a man of standing in your community, even if you do not make the White House. And who can tell? Maybe that also."

—*On Growing Up*

To the question, what did he enjoy most while President?
"The thing I enjoyed most were visits from children. They did not want public offices."

—*On Growing Up*

To the question, What are you doing now? (1961)
"I am busy writing books on history. I believe in that old saying, 'Those who do not remember the past are condemned to relive it.'"

—*On Growing Up*

MEMORABLE EVENTS
DURING HOOVER'S LIFE

1874   Herbert Hoover born, August 10, West Branch, Iowa.

1878   First commercial telephone exchanges opened.

1881   President James A. Garfield shot. Chester Alan Arthur became President.

1895   Hoover was graduated with pioneer class, Leland Stanford Junior University.

1899   Herbert Hoover married Lou Henry, February 10, Monterey, California.

1900   Boxer Rebellion. Hoovers in siege of Tientsin.

1901   President McKinley shot. Theodore Roosevelt became President.

1903   First automobile trip across U.S. Henry Ford organized Ford Motor Company. First airplane flight by Wright Brothers.

1911   First transcontinental airplane flight.

1912   Woodrow Wilson elected President.

1914   Ford Motor Company raised wages from $2.40 for nine-hour day to $5.00 for eight-hour day. First ship through the Panama Canal. Outbreak of World War I. Hoover undertook to direct Commission for Relief of Belgium.

1915   First telephone conversation New York to San Francisco.

1917   U.S. entered World War I. Hoover became Food Administrator. Revolution overturned Russian Empire. Provisional government established. Russia taken over by Bolshevist Revolution.

1918 Armistice ended World War I, November 11.

1919 Treaty of Versailles. Eighteenth (Prohibition) Amendment passed in U.S.

1920 League of Nations formed without U.S. membership. Warren G. Harding elected President. Nineteenth (Universal Suffrage) Amendment went into effect in U.S.

1921 Herbert Hoover became Secretary of Commerce.

1923 U.S. Steel abandoned 84-hour week. Harding died. Calvin Coolidge became President.

1924 Hoover opened negotiations with Canada about St. Lawrence Waterway. Woodrow Wilson died.

1927 Charles A. Lindbergh flew solo nonstop flight to Paris. Great Mississippi flood.

1928 Hoover elected President. Big Bull Market.

1929 Wall Street crash. Beginning of Great Depression.

1930 Establishment of Pan American Airways. Work begun on Hoover Dam. First airmail to Brazil and Argentina.

1931 Withdrawal of American Marines from Nicaragua and Haiti. Establishment of Good Neighbor Policy with Latin America.

1933 Franklin D. Roosevelt inaugurated President. Adolph Hitler became Chancellor of Germany. Germany quit League of Nations. FDR recognized Soviet government of Russia. Prohibition ended.

1934 Hitler became Fuehrer.

1935 Hitler rejected Versailles Treaty, began to rearm.

1938 Hitler invaded Austria.

1939 World War II began.

1941 Hoover Tower dedicated at Stanford University, to house Institution on War, Revolution and Peace. U.S. went to war against Japan after attack on U.S. Fleet at Pearl Harbor.

1944   Lou Henry Hoover died, January 7.

1945   Franklin D. Roosevelt died in fourth term. Harry Truman became President. U.N. adopted charter in San Francisco. First atomic bomb dropped on Hiroshima, August 6. World War II ended.

1946   Hoover made world food survey for President Truman.

1947   Hoover headed Economic Mission to Germany and Austria. Hoover appointed to head commission on Organization of Executive branch of Government: The Hoover Commission.

1949   Hoover seventy-five years old. Public recognition.

1950   United States at war with Korea.

1952   Dwight D. Eisenhower elected President.

1953   Hoover directed work of Second Hoover Commission. Korean armistice signed.

1956   Civil Rights demands and demonstrations begin with Montgomery, Alabama, bus boycott.

1957   First man-made satellite, Sputnik, sent into orbit by U.S.S.R.

1958   First satellite launched by United States, Explorer I. U.S. jet airline passenger service opened.

1959   Castro took over Cuba. Opening of the St. Lawrence Seaway.

1960   John F. Kennedy elected President.

1963   President Kennedy assassinated in Dallas. Lyndon B. Johnson became President.

1964   Herbert Hoover died in New York City, October 20. Buried in West Branch, Iowa.

FOR FURTHER READING

Herbert Hoover speaks for himself:

MEMOIRS OF HERBERT HOOVER. 3 volumes. The Macmillan Company, New York, 1951-1952
Hoover tells his own story from his boyhood through the Presidency. The years of his mining experiences and of the First World War are especially interesting.

HOOVER AFTER DINNER. Charles Scribner's Sons, New York, 1933
The speeches he made to the Gridiron Club about fishing, politics, and the problems of being a President, always with a light touch and humor.

ON GROWING UP. William Morrow and Company, New York, 1962.
His letters to children who wrote him, telling them about his first job, his own hero, how to become President, pets, and answering other questions they asked.

ADDRESSES UPON THE AMERICAN ROAD. Scribner, 1938-1941; Van Nostrand, New York, 1946-1949; Stanford University Press, California, 1951-1955; Caxton Press, Caldwell, Idaho, 1961.
There are several volumes of these addresses—all the speeches, broadcasts, messages, and articles he gave and wrote during the years following his Presidency. They contain his philosophy, his humor, his hopes for his country, and his firm faith in the American way of freedom.

AMERICAN INDIVIDUALISM. Doubleday Page, New York, 1922

He wrote this small book when he came back from witnessing the tragedies of World War I, telling what individualism means in spiritual stature, self-respect, and freedom.

FISHING FOR FUN. Random House, New York, 1963

Light-hearted comments about fishing, its rewards and its frustrations, by one of its leading sportsmen.

As others saw Herbert Hoover:

HERBERT HOOVER: A REMINISCENT BIOGRAPHY by Will Irwin. The Century Company, New York, 1928

A friend from college days writes about a friend he knew well and admired.

HERBERT HOOVER, AMERICAN QUAKER by David Hinshaw. Farrar, Straus and Giroux, New York, 1950

David Hinshaw was also a long-time friend from the early years.

HOOVER OFF THE RECORD by Theodore G. Joslin. Doubleday, Doran and Co., 1934

Mr. Joslin was one of Mr. Hoover's secretaries during the Presidency. He records an inside view of the President's work, the demands upon him, and the man in office.

HERBERT HOOVER: A BIOGRAPHY by Eugene Lyons. Doubleday and Company, New York, 1964

This is the most nearly complete story of Hoover, by a man who came to know him in the later years. Many interesting details of this exceptionally full life, which could not be included in *American Friend*, are told in this book.

ACKNOWLEDGMENTS

I wish to express my appreciation to Mrs. Charles A. McLean, daughter of Herbert Hoover's brother, Theodore, who provided me with a copy of the geneology of the Hoover family; to the estate of Herbert Hoover for permission to quote from his writings; and to the publisher and others who permitted quotations from published materials and supplied pictures, as follows: from *The Memoirs of Herbert Hoover, Vol. I* by Herbert Hoover, copyright 1951 by Herbert Hoover, the quotations on pages 45, 53, 73, 76, 83, 92, 100, 109, and 201; from *The Memoirs of Herbert Hoover, Vol. II* by Herbert Hoover, copyright 1951, 1952 by Herbert Hoover, the quotations on pages 115, 117, 126, 129, 133, and 142; from *The Memoirs of Herbert Hoover, Vol. III* by Herbert Hoover, copyright 1952 by Herbert Hoover, the quotations on pages 159-160, 164, 168, 188, 189, and 208 (letter), all by permission of The Macmillan Company; from *Herbert Hoover: A Biography*, by Eugene Lyons, copyright 1948, 1964 by Eugene Lyons; copyright 1947 by Reader's Digest Association, Inc., the quotations on pages 11, 20, 21, 26, 27, 111, 202, 208 (beginning on line 27), 212 (line 13) reprinted by permission of Doubleday & Company, Inc.; from *Our Times by Mark Sullivan, Vol. V*, the quotations on pages 104 and 119 (beginning line 21) from *The Hoover Administration* by William S. Myers and Walter H. Newton, the quotations on pages 170, 171, and the one cited on page 216; from *Addresses Upon the American Road* and *Challenge to Liberty* by Herbert Hoover, those cited on page 215, all by permission of Charles Scribner's Sons; from *On Growing Up: His Letters from and to American Children* by Herbert Hoover, copyright 1949, 1959, 1962 by Herbert Hoover, those cited on pages 216 and 217, by permission of William Morrow & Company, Inc.; from *Herbert Hoover's Home Town* by Maud Stratton, the quotation on page 17, by permission of Mrs. Donald Daut, Mrs. Robert Witmer, and Mrs. H. L. Witmer; from *Fishing for Fun* by Herbert Hoover, copyright 1963, the quotation on page 119 beginning on line 6, by permission of Random House, Inc.; from *The World at Home* by Anne O'Hare McCormick, the quotation on page 169 by permission of Alfred A. Knopf, Incorporated; from *Herbert Hoover, American Quaker* by David Hinshaw, the quotations on pages 198, 209, by permission of Farrar, Straus & Giroux, Inc.; from *The Palimpsest*, by permission of The State Historical Society of Iowa, the quotations on pages 212 (sixth line from the end) and 214. The quotations on pages 143 and 166 are from *Hoover Off the Record* by Theodore Joslin and those on pages 195 and 216 are from *Hoover After Dinner* by Theodore Joslin.

The picture on page 15 is used by courtesy of Mildred Speight of West Branch, Iowa; those on pages 34, 35, and 36 are from the Newsom Collection, recently acquired by the Hoover Memorial Library; those on pages 184 and 185 are used by courtesy of *The Chicago Tribune;* the one on page 190 is used by permission of Headquarters, 140th Aviation Battalion, Long Beach, California; the picture on page 199 is reprinted by permission of Compix; all others are from the Hoover Memorial Library, West Branch, Iowa (the one on page 13 is a photograph by Signor Larson).

INDEX

PRINTED IN U.S.A.